OVEREATERS ANONYMOUS

OVEREATERS ANONYMOUS

Overeaters Anonymous, Inc.
Torrance, California

ISBN: 0-9609898-1-1

Library of Congress Catalog Card No.: 80-50589

Overeaters Anonymous
2190 190th Street, Torrance, California 90504

Contents

Foreword

I HAVE HAD BOTH A personal and professional interest in obesity for a great many years. The fact is I've been an overeater all of my life and a fat man most of my life. I did not understand the destructive aspects of overeating, however, until I began to practice psychiatry.

Eventually it became apparent to me that overeating is an obsessive, compulsive addiction of a highly complex nature. I became aware that food can be even more addictive than tobacco, drugs, alcohol or gambling, and at least as destructive. The simple fact is that we cannot do without food and each time the food addict eats he or she is in danger of succumbing to the compulsion.

The further facts are:

    1. Food is usually available in abundance.

2. There is no societal, legal dictum against eating.
3. In many places overeating is encouraged.
4. Confusion about this highly complex syndrome abounds.

Indeed, there is still a great deal we do not know about overeating. But we do know now that one's emotional life has a great deal to do with overeating. I believe that repressed anger plays a powerful role in this addiction. I feel that eating binges are often displaced temper tantrums or rage reactions. I also believe that the roots of the condition can often be traced to the earliest times in our lives and to early and complicated family relations. Those who suffer from the problem and those who seriously engage in working in the area also know how malignant the condition is. This destructive aspect occurs relative to the victim's physical health, emotional wellbeing, social life, professional life, sex life and economic life.

We also know, unfortunately, how limited all treatment modalities have been to date in effecting sustained relief, let alone "cures." We know, too, how obese people have been patronized, prejudiced against and exploited for economic gain. Charlatans and chicanery abound. Millions of dollars are made off the suffering of fat people, and this condition is probably the most prevalent health problem which exists in the American population. Of course, as with all other problems, there are varying degrees of difficulty and suffering. But the numbers of people who are driven to seek help make commercial enterprise in this field big business.

Overeaters Anonymous is not a business. This organization represents one of our country's major and perhaps largest efforts at self-help — real and effective self-help. OA enjoys a reputation for significant success in a field strewn with failure. OA's success goes beyond weight reduction and control, though this alone is an achievement of great magnitude. OA also helps to contribute a greater sense of self and self-esteem through its extraordinary implementation of camaraderie and caring for one's fellows and one's self. It functions as a giant contributor to awakening and adding to its members' sense of their own humanity. This is crucial in battling malignant addiction or, for that matter, any illness of the mind and body; they really are one.

This book describes the OA experience as told by various members through their own stories. These are moving and educational stories. They are full of struggle — constructive struggle — and hope. Most important, they tell of enhanced compassion for self, for others and for the state of being human. They tell us about fellowship and what a powerful therapeutic instrument caring can be. They also tell us what caring is all about. Read them and enjoy being part of the human condition.

THEODORE ISAAC RUBIN, M.D.

Dr. Rubin is a well-known psychoanalyst and president of the American Institute for Psychoanalysis. He serves on a dozen local and national medical boards and is the author of more than twenty books, including the widely acclaimed *David and Lisa* and *Compassion and Self-Hate*. Among the many honors he has won are the Adolph Meyer Award from the Association for the Improvement of Mental Health and the Social Conscience Award from the Karen Horney Clinic, a psychiatric institution.

Acknowledgment

*T*HIS BOOK WOULD not be possible without our great preceptor, Alcoholics Anonymous. Indeed, many of those whose contributions appear in these pages would not be among us today without the steps and traditions of the AA program.

In publishing this collection of personal stories of recovery, Overeaters Anonymous has only one purpose: to describe for all who may be interested the progression of our illness, what we found in this program and how it has changed us. Our book is not intended as a substitute for or a replacement of *Alcoholics Anonymous*, the life-giving "Big Book" which has brought physical, emotional and spiritual rebirth to millions around the globe.

Those of us who speak in these pages confirm the prophetic words used in 1951 in conferring the Lasker Award on the then sixteen-year-old Fellowship of Alcoholics Anonymous:

" . . . Historians may one day recognize Alcoholics Anonymous to have been a great venture in social pioneering which forged a new instrument for social action; a new therapy based on the kinship of common suffering; one having a vast potential for the myriad other ills of mankind."

Our deepest gratitude to the Fellowship of Alcoholics Anonymous for their continued growth without promotion, exemplary leadership without leaders and principles without personalities.

OVEREATERS
ANONYMOUS

Our Invitation To You

WE OF OVEREATERS ANONYMOUS have made a discovery. At the very first meeting we attended, we learned that we were in the clutches of a dangerous illness, and that willpower, emotional health and self-confidence, which some of us had once possessed, were no defense against it.

To be sure, the picture painted of the disease was grim: progressive, debilitating, incurable. Compulsive overeating has many symptoms in addition to mere fat. It is also an illness which isolates and gradually, or rapidly, causes increasingly serious problems in one or more areas of our lives: health, job, finances, family or social life.

No one is sure what causes it; probably a number of factors: environment, a certain way of reacting to life, biological predisposition.

1

We have learned that the reasons are unimportant. What deserves the attention of the still-suffering compulsive overeater is this: *there is a proven, workable method by which we can arrest our illness.*

The OA recovery program is identical with that of Alcoholics Anonymous. We use AA's twelve steps and twelve traditions, changing only the words "alcohol" and "alcoholic" to "food" and "compulsive overeater."

As the personal stories in this book attest, the twelve-step program of recovery works as well for compulsive overeaters as it does for alcoholics. Our rapidly increasing numbers* prove that compulsive overeaters can share their problems and help each other, thus benefiting not only themselves but their families and the communities in which they live.

Can we guarantee *you* this recovery? The answer is simple. If you will honestly face the truth about yourself and the illness; if you will keep coming back to meetings to talk and listen to other recovering compulsive overeaters; if you will read our literature and that of Alcoholics Anonymous with an open mind; and, most important, if you are willing to rely on a power greater than yourself for direction in your life, and to take the twelve steps to the best of your ability, we believe you can indeed join the ranks of those who recover.

The disease of compulsive overeating causes or contributes to illness on three levels — emotional, physical and spiritual. To remedy this threefold illness we offer several suggestions, but the reader should keep in mind that the basis of the program is spiritual, as evidenced by the twelve steps.

We are not a "diet and calories" club. We do not endorse any particular plan of eating. We practice absti-

---

*In January 1980, there were some 100,000 members in more than 4,800 groups in 24 countries.

nence by staying away from all eating between planned meals and from all individual binge foods. Once we become abstinent, the preoccupation with food diminishes and in many cases leaves us entirely. We then find that, to deal with our inner turmoil, we have to have a new way of thinking, of acting on life rather than reacting to it — in essence, a new way of living.

From this vantage point, we begin the twelve-step program of recovery, moving beyond the food and the emotional havoc to a fuller living experience.

We believe that no amount of willpower or self-determination could have saved us. Times without number, our resolutions and plans were shattered as we saw our individual resources fail.

So we honestly admitted to ourselves that we were powerless over food. This was the first step toward recovery. It followed that, if we had no power of our own, we needed a power outside ourselves to help us recover.

Some of us, including agnostics and atheists, regard the group itself as a power greater than ourselves. Others choose to accept different interpretations of this power. But most of us adopt the concept of God as God may be understood by each individual.

As a result of practicing the steps, the symptom of compulsive overeating is removed on a daily basis. Thus, for most of us, abstinence means freedom from the bondage of compulsive overeating, achieved through the process of surrendering to something greater than ourselves; the more total our surrender, the more fully realized our freedom from food obsession.

Here are the steps as adapted for Overeaters Anonymous:

1. We admitted we were powerless over food — that our lives had become unmanageable.
2. Came to believe that a Power greater than ourselves could restore us to sanity.
3. Made a decision to turn our will and our lives over to the care of God *as we understood Him*.
4. Made a searching and fearless moral inventory of ourselves.
5. Admitted to God, to ourselves and to another human being the exact nature of our wrongs.
6. Were entirely ready to have God remove all these defects of character.
7. Humbly asked Him to remove our shortcomings.
8. Made a list of all persons we had harmed, and became willing to make amends to them all.
9. Made direct amends to such people wherever possible, except when to do so would injure them or others.
10. Continued to take personal inventory and when we were wrong, promptly admitted it.
11. Sought through prayer and meditation to improve our conscious contact with God *as we understood Him*, praying only for knowledge of His will for us and the power to carry that out.
12. Having had a spiritual awakening as the result of these steps, we tried to carry this message to compulsive overeaters and to practice these principles in all our affairs.*

"How can I face this?" you may ask. We suggest you do so only one day at a time. "Just for today" is one of many deeply meaningful OA slogans. "I can do anything for twenty-four hours that I couldn't do for a

---

*Reprinted by permission of AA World Services, Inc.

lifetime" was a brand new way of thinking for us. Before, we looked at our weight problem — and all our other problems — and said, "What's the use? It's too much for me. I can't possibly do it."

Now, we fully accept and live by the premise that we don't have to look at everything all at once. We know that it's necessary to do a certain amount of planning but, once having planned, we act for this one day alone.

"But I'm too weak. I'll never make it!" Don't worry; we have all thought and said the same thing. The amazing secret to the success of this program is just that: weakness. It is weakness, not strength, that binds us to each other and to a higher power and somehow gives us an ability to do what we cannot do alone. We have discovered that if people in this program love us, it is not for our strength, but for our weakness and our willingness to share that with others.

After reading the personal stories in this book, you may proclaim, "I'm not *that* bad!" Once again, we ask you to keep in mind that compulsive overeating is a progressive illness. If you really are a compulsive overeater, the symptoms will grow worse. Within our ranks are those who were recovering but tried once again to control food by their own devices, with consequent return to serious overeating and, in many cases, massive weight gain.

If you can identify with the developing pattern of overeating revealed in our stories, you probably are a compulsive overeater. The chances are that your symptoms will eventually reach those of late-stage compulsive overeating. In other words, you're not that bad — yet!

If, after reading this book, you decide you are one of us, we welcome you with open arms. You are not alone any more! Overeaters Anonymous extends to all of you the gift of acceptance. No matter who you are, where you come from or where you are going, you are welcome here. Regardless of what you have done or failed to do, what you have felt or haven't felt, who you have loved or hated, you may be sure of our unconditional acceptance.

We will help you and rejoice with you and tell you that we are not failures just because we sometimes fail. We'll hold out our arms in love and stand beside you as you pull yourself back up and walk on again to where you are heading.

Sometimes *we* fail to be all that we could be, and sometimes we aren't there to give you all you need from us. Accept our imperfections, too. Love and help us in return. That is what we are in OA — imperfect but progressing. Let us rejoice together in our recovery and in the assurance that we have a home, if we want it.

Welcome to Overeaters Anonymous. Welcome home!

1

Keep Coming Back
Rozanne's Story

*H*ONEY, IF YOU have a twenty-three inch waist, everything else will be all right."

My mother's words were to haunt me all my growing-up years. The promise that a slender figure would bring instant and permanent happiness was an illusion in which I believed with all my heart and soul.

The few times I was thin, nothing else changed. I figured that the fault was mine, and if I tried harder, the world would be different. The persistence of my illusion was astonishing.

Trying harder was a family tradition. I come from a family of superachievers, almost all of them compulsive overeaters. My mother grew up in Green Bay, Wisconsin where my grandfather owned the first movie theater and had the first car in that small town. My grandmother was very daring: she worked

7

with Margaret Sanger in the early days of Planned Parenthood. Both my parents were extremely education-oriented. Thus, only a grade of "A" was welcome. "B" was tolerable, but a "C" was just not acceptable. So my brother and I learned early that the way to be worth anything was to work very hard and to achieve beyond the scope of most other people. Just being a loving human being wasn't enough; we had to be able to produce to be worthwhile.

I decided early that if I was going to produce, I would be noticed for my efforts. I discovered that I loved being in the forefront the first time I led the kindergarten band. I have never forgotten turning around after the performance, hearing the applause and bowing to the audience. After that, I was hooked. I wanted desperately to be an actress, because that way I would be noticed. I studied drama for many years; I was on the school debating team and editor of the school newspaper. I lived in Chicago, where the opportunities were excellent, and I took advantage of all of them.

Unfortunately, during all this time, I was very plump. So many times I heard well-meaning people say, "You have such a pretty face, dear. If only you'd lose weight." That used to break my heart. Did it mean I wasn't any good because I was fat? I just tried a little harder, worked a little more, studied a little longer.

But none of it had any effect. You see, I had a secret I told no one. I hated myself. I was convinced that I was no good. I carried that feeling all through my life, and no amount of superachieving could wipe it out.

Still, I kept on trying. I was a good student, my grades were high, and I became such a good girl that I became "teacher's pet." That last destroyed my relationships with the other children, but it was all I had.

It was the only assurance that I might be worth something to another human being.

I was eighteen and in my third year at the University of Chicago when I made a decision to give up overeating. The motivation was boys. I wanted to date, and it was obvious that being fat was never going to get me any phone calls. So I went on a diet, and for the first time in my life I was thin. I was 5'2" and weighed 118 pounds.

Suddenly, the boys began to notice me. I had so many dates, I began to neglect my studies and flunked every subject, disgracing my family. I was sent to a business school where I not only learned my lesson but some useful vocational skills as well. The following year I returned to put myself through the University and earn a degrée.

When I was twenty-one, I moved to New York City to find fame and fortune in the theater. It was not long before I realized that actors, having to make frequent rounds to audition for roles, were subject to constant rejections. I saw that this was no life for me. My fear of rejection was so strong that it overrode any ambitions I had. I settled for working behind the scenes as a producer's secretary, where it was safe.

It was an exciting life. Unfortunately, I had long since regained my weight. And I still hated myself. In addition, I had developed a fierce resentment toward my mother. I now blamed her for my unhappiness.

After returning home to Chicago where I worked as a fashion copywriter for a period, I decided to make another change. "I'm going to California," I told my parents, "to find a job and a husband."

In Los Angeles, I again went to great lengths to find a man: I gave up food and became thin once more. After another copywriting stint, I became assistant ad manager of a small chain of department stores. I loved it. I met a marvelous man, and life really seemed to be going my way.

But I was still plagued by self-hate. I was hanging onto the diet by the skin of my teeth. The motivation (finding a man) enabled me to diet for a time. When Marvin proposed to me, I weighed 118 pounds, and at our wedding four months later, I weighed 129. All it took was that little ring on my finger for me to take back the food.

Within three years of our marriage, we had two little girls. By this time, life was too much for me. I was up to 148 pounds, I couldn't stop eating and most of the time I wished I were dead. My self-worth was completely gone, my soul was empty, I had no place to go and I didn't believe in God. What was left for me?

The answer came one quiet November night in 1958. I was watching Paul Coates, a syndicated television columnist, interview a member from a new organization called Gamblers Anonymous. My husband had a friend who was a compulsive gambler, and I thought this might be just the thing for him. So Marvin and I took his friend to a GA meeting just before Thanksgiving.

As long as I live, I will never forget that night. We were in a meeting hall with about twenty-five men and a sprinkling of wives. Each man in turn got up and talked about his life of lying and cheating and stealing. I sat there transfixed. "My God," I thought, "I'm not alone, after all." The room became brighter and brighter, and I wanted to cry with relief. I was not the only one; there were others who felt as I felt and who had done what I had done! Of course, our compulsions were not the same. They were obsessed with gambling and money, and I thought of nothing but overeating and food. Still, inside we were the same. When I walked out of the meeting room that night, my life changed forever.

I managed to stay on a diet for three weeks, but as usual, I couldn't hang on by myself and went back to my old ways. I ate and cried the whole next year, until Christmas found me at a new high of 161 pounds. I was terrified. What was I to do? Where could I go? I had tried suicide in my late teens, and I'd had several years of conventional therapy. It had not helped my eating problem.

I felt my world was coming to an end. There was just one weight-control organization available at the time, and it wasn't listed in the phone book. I was frantic.

Then I remembered Gamblers Anonymous. I told my husband I was going back to see if they could help me form an organization like theirs for compulsive overeaters like me.

By the winter of 1959, GA was two and a half years old and doing very well. The meeting I attended was still comprised only of men, but they welcomed me warmly. After the meeting, I approached Jim W., the founder of GA. My heart was pounding; I felt my whole life was at stake.

"Jim," I asked, "do you think an organization like yours could work for compulsive overeaters like me?"

He smiled at me and replied, "Why, I don't see why not. I was in Alcoholics Anonymous before I ever started GA. What can I do to help?"

There it was — a hand outstretched to steady me as I stumbled along! It was my first experience with the twelfth step, the first time anyone had offered to help me with no thought of return. I went home and told Marvin, "I think I finally have a chance!" That evening, we found a name for the yet-unborn organization: Overeaters Anonymous.

With my usual self-willed zeal, I sailed into saving

the world. Unfortunately, all the twenty-five or thirty women I approached had one excuse or another for not joining me in this marvelous enterprise. I did not realize that I was preaching at them, telling them what a great idea this was for solving their very evident problem.

One crisp January day I was walking down the street with my very overweight neighbor, chatting as we both pushed our babies in strollers. I remember telling her about *my* problem and *my* solution, never once intimating that she had the same problem. Finally, she was so intrigued, she coaxed me into telling her the name of the organization. I told her, then said, "But I know you won't be interested."

"Oh yes, I am," she said. "I think I need it, too." At that moment, the Fellowship of Overeaters Anonymous was born.

On January 19, 1960 we held the first OA meeting. Jo and I were there, along with Bernice K., the wife of a GA member. Bernice left at the third meeting, explaining, "My doctor says dieting makes me nervous." With that, she walked out the door. Jo and I looked at each other. I said, "Dieting makes me nervous, too." Jo wanted to leave, but I started to cry and said that I couldn't do it alone and she had to stay. She did.

We struggled along. I had been to two GA meetings; Jo had never been to any Anonymous meeting. We both lost a lot of weight. She went from 197 pounds to 109 by August, and I went from 161 to 110 in the same time. Physically, we were great programs of attraction. My feelings of worthlessness, however, were in full swing. The less I ate, the more all my anxieties rose to the surface. I managed to cover them with a good deal of self-will.

The first thing I decided was that those AA steps were very poorly written. I felt that Bill W., who with

Dr. Bob had founded AA, was only a stockbroker, and, after all, I was a professional writer. Besides, I believed that I was not so weak that I had to turn my life and my will over to the care of any God, whether he existed or not. Thus, I removed step three. In its place I wrote a step advocating consultation with "a physician of our own choosing." I was so adamant (and frightened) that I proceeded to remove the word "God" and all mention of spiritual concepts from the rest of the steps. Then I took a good look at what I had done and realized that the steps didn't look at all like AA's.

"After all," I thought, "I do want people to say we are like AA." So I sparingly sprinkled God back into some of the steps.

None of us knew any better. After a couple of months, there were Jo and myself and five of Jo's friends. Nobody in the group had ever been to AA, and I was the only one who had gone to GA. So we sat around and talked about our feelings in a very psychological manner. We knew nothing of the meaning of inventories or amends, and I bristled at the very thought of surrender and spiritual awakening.

Finally, Jim suggested that we visit an AA meeting. "Oh, I couldn't," I shot back. "They might be drunk and accost us." Oh, the patience of Jim!

"No," he replied, "the drunks are many other places, but the sober ones are in the AA meetings." So, with fear and trembling, the seven of us went to Alcoholics Anonymous open meetings. What an eye-opening experience that was! I listened to concepts I had never heard before, and I experienced a tangible love in the room. Later on, AA members were to be a great source of sharing and support for us. But that night, my fears were in the way; I was still unable to accept many of the basic precepts of the AA program.

I had very little understanding of what it was like to have my compulsive nature removed, so I turned to compulsive spending. I rationalized by saying that now I had a new figure so I simply had to have a lot of new clothes. I later learned this was just a coverup for my real feelings. That emptiness in my soul that I had tried to fill with men (before my marriage), food and possessions was a spiritual emptiness. But I didn't understand it then; I didn't believe in God. The thinner I became, the more I achieved, the worse I felt. I couldn't let people know this, though. They might find out how rotten I was.

In the summer of 1960 a television interview brought in five hundred letters, and Overeaters Anonymous was on its way! My own troubles, however, were just beginning. I was not overeating, I was thin, I was spending compulsively — and I was a mass of self-will run riot. I felt because I had been one of OA's founders that every word I uttered was a pearl of wisdom. I believed that everyone had to listen to me. That was the only way I could make myself important. I couldn't achieve that feeling from inside, and I simply didn't know what to do.

In trying to get me to reinstate step three, Jim W. explained that I needed to admit that I could not stop eating by myself, that I was "willpowerless" over food and that I needed help. His gentle suggestion opened the door to spiritual belief for me. I didn't step over the threshold then, however. My Higher Power was the group and the individuals in OA.

The resentment toward my mother, which I carried for twenty-five years, was corroding my very core. At a sponsor's prodding, I made amends to my parents. They lived in another city, so I had to write to them. I took the letter to the mailbox and dropped it in. As I turned to walk away, I heard the clank of the mailbox door. With that sound, twenty-five years of resentment disappeared. In one brief moment, everything was gone! I could hardly believe it; that was one of the most miraculous things I had ever experienced.

In July 1964, after several inventories, I took one specifically on compulsive spending. On July 30, when I brought the inventory to my sponsor's house, I weighed 109½ pounds. I walked out of there knowing that I would never spend like that again. And I walked right into a family party, took that first bite and continued to overeat. By March 1973, I weighed 185 pounds.

I was still swinging from one compulsion to another. Somehow, the essence of the program was eluding me. I resigned from the OA office, though I continued to attend meetings. I took inventories, cried on the phone, went to meetings — and continued to overeat. What was wrong?

I kept coming back to meetings, sitting in the back of the room with my big, black coat wrapped around me. I felt hopeless and desolate, unable to make a phone call when I wanted to eat. Compulsive overeating is a disease of isolation, and my paralyzing inability to call was part of my illness. At one meeting, I managed to ask for help, and a wonderful woman called me for four months before I was able to call back.

The next three years were a great learning experience for me. I found that the reactions of others to me were caused in part by their fear of having the same thing happen to them. Of course, my flailing about and striking out didn't help my relationships at all. Slowly, I lost 30 pounds. Incomprehensible demoralization was still a part of my daily life. But I kept coming back, and I certainly learned a lot about patience.

Praying for guidance, I did expect a miracle. In De-

cember 1976, that miracle happened. I was sitting in a
Big Book study group. The leader began paraphrasing
the first sentence of Chapter Three: "Most of us were
unwilling to admit that we were real compulsive
overeaters."

I felt as though someone had hit me right in the pit
of the stomach. Suddenly, I knew what was wrong
with me. I had not fully conceded to my innermost
self that I was a compulsive overeater. I had not taken
that vital first step toward recovery. The leader continued, "No real overeater ever recovers control." All
those years during which I had read that book, I never
saw the word "control." For some reason, I believed
that none of us could recover. Yet Chapter Five in the
same book suggests the steps as "a program of recovery." The promise of recovery, a daily reprieve from
my illness, gave me hope. The certain knowledge that
I could never control my overeating gave me a chance
at recovery at last.

But I still had no self-worth. One day, I heard a
woman say, "I tried to tell myself, 'Mary, you're OK,'
and I couldn't say it in front of a mirror. It took me six
months to do it."

I took this as a challenge and decided that what
took her six months to do I could do immediately. I
tried to tell myself I was OK, and I started to cry. And
I couldn't stop crying. So I remembered my sponsors'
lessons. They had taught me to "act as if." They told
me that I didn't have to want to, or like it or believe it.
They emphasized that I must take the action, and the
feelings would follow.

Acting as if it were true, I practiced telling myself,
"Rozanne, you're OK." Unable to look at myself in the
mirror, I said this all day, every day for six months.
Then, one wondrous December evening, I was all
dressed up to go out. I was in a hurry and paused

briefly to check myself in the hall mirror as I prepared to rush out the door. And then I really stopped. I looked at myself, smiled and said, "Rozanne, you're OK. You are one fantastic lady, and I love you."

Today, my body is once more a normal size. I can care about others because I care about myself. Because I kept coming back, I learned the validity of an elementary spiritual principle given to me by the Reverend Rollo M. Boas, one of OA's earliest friends whose comments grace this book: "If you remove your body from the truth, when you are ready the truth is nowhere to be found. But if you continue to bring your body to the truth, then when you are ready the truth is waiting there for you."

And that truth — our promise of recovery — is in every OA meeting when we join hands, pray together and joyously, lovingly encourage one another: Keep Coming Back!

2

The Man Who Came To Visit

*I*T IS HARD TO BELIEVE that I was once an incubator baby. My parents were of the old country belief that "a fat baby is a healthy baby." I grew healthier and healthier. From "He's such a big baby, God bless him" to "Look how cute and chubby he is" and eventually, "Oh my God, look how fat he is!"

I'll start my story with "Look how fat he is!" Asking a girl out at the age of seventeen was fun: all of them seemed to be booked up for months. All, that is, except the honest ones. They told me I was too fat. I bought what friends I had. Food, drugs, money, a place to hold a party — anything I knew they needed, they got.

When I was alone, which was quite often, I would sit in my room, read books, eat large amounts of food, watch television and have constant thoughts of suicide. My parents thought I had a problem so I was

carted off to therapists, psychologists, psychiatrists
and play therapy. All because of my depressions, my
antisocial behavior, my eating, my drinking and —
worst of all — my use of drugs. It was OK that I was fat
and that I stole booze from my father's closet, but the
last straw was when they found out about my opium
addiction.

Why not? How many times can a person stand on the
side when teams are chosen and not get picked? How
many rejections can one take? How could I continue to
buy people and not have it take its toll? The food
soothed the hurt I felt inside, the alcohol bolstered my
nonexistent ego and the opium made it all seem to go
away.

As I grew older I began to handle my problems better
— or was it that I just ignored them? I met a woman
who shared many of my interests: food, art, drugs and
the deep incessant need to be loved and accepted.

Her father owned a restaurant, I loved to cook and
we got high on grass together. We were both quite
overweight but that was OK — we had each other. We
were married seven months after we met and went to
Montreal on our honeymoon. We spent a week at the
best hotels, ate the best foods and had a beautiful time.
We spent more than one thousand dollars that week,
only three hundred of which was in hotel bills. How
could two people spend more than seven hundred dollars on food in one week? With two compulsive overeaters it was easy, it was divine, it was disgusting.

I gained 25 pounds that week and couldn't fit into
my tuxedo. I gained weight every week after that,
maybe a pound or two but it kept adding up until I decided to do something about it. I found diet pills. They
worked fine for two days. I came home on my lunch
hour, cleaned the house, made the bed, did the dishes
and ate lunch. The pills soon enabled me to eat faster

— and more. I continued to gain weight. I tried diets I
found in books and magazines: egg, grapefruit, ice
cream, water and even the drinking man's diet. I tried
doctors' diets, military diets, hospital diets and com-
binations from all of them. They worked for awhile —
one or two weeks, maybe even a month.

Then came the commercial weight groups: sign in,
lay down your weekly fee, get on the scale, listen to the
lecturer and then go out and eat your face in. It was OK
because I would fast two days before the next meeting.

We moved out of New York City and into the country,
thinking the change would do us good. It did. We immediately found a restaurant that delivered.

"Yes, I would like to order four special Italian din-
ners, two large antipastos, three garlic breads, two
quarts of ices and a large diet soda." The rationale of
the diet soda still escapes me. This was a dinner for two
people, and what we didn't finish right away was gone
by morning. The gremlins took it; they had to because I
denied sneaking into the kitchen and so did my wife.
Since we were the only two people there, it had to be
gremlins or perhaps the food fairy.

Time passed, weight was lost and weight was
gained. Diets came and went, hundreds of dollars were
spent on doctors and food, pills and food, food and
more food. I gave up. I resigned myself to spending the
rest of my life as a drunk and as a fatty. Our minds are
fantastic; eventually I began to think that I didn't have
a weight problem. I held my weight well.

My mother told my wife about a new program that
she was in and how it was working for her. My wife was
ready for it, but in our area it was nowhere to be found.
So she waited. A year later she heard about a group
that met about forty miles away from our home. At 300
pounds-plus she was willing to try anything, so she
went to this new diet group, this new way of life that

my mother had found. I wasn't ready. I didn't have a weight problem. I didn't need it. She went, and said it was great and that it was helping her. That was OK for her, but look what it was doing to my telephone bill. All those long distance calls, the phone ringing at all hours of the night, the times I had to leave the room while she was on the phone so she could have privacy.

After a month of all this secrecy I was invited to come to the meeting to watch her "step up." Sure, she lost weight and was calm and serene and accepted my eating and drinking, but I wasn't ready for what she had. I went to the meeting that night to make her happy because I loved her.

Walking into a room filled with more than one hundred women in various stages of fat and various ranges of thin was a new experience. Then came the holding hands and the incantations, the stories of past horrors and present joys, the revelations of spiritual experiences. These were all crazy people. I didn't need any of this. At the break, people came up to me and asked if I needed a sponsor or if I was new in the program. I was just visiting, thanks, I didn't have a weight problem.

Soon the program began seeping its way into my thoughts. I realized that I should go on a diet of some sort. After all, I did weigh more than 275 pounds and no matter how well I carried my weight it had to show. Yet I still wanted some control; I wanted to eat what I wanted when I wanted it and as much as I wanted.

My spiritual awakening and my rock bottom came when I was at my parents' home alone. I was hungry (as usual) and decided to raid the fridge. I came upon a frozen cake: "Thaw at room temperature two to three hours." They had to be kidding. I couldn't wait two to three minutes, let alone hours. I popped it in the oven at 500 degrees and checked it every two minutes. After ten minutes it wasn't thawed out. I took a knife and fork and began chipping away at this frozen mass, angry that only a small piece at a time could be gotten into my mouth. I chipped harder, hoping that larger chunks would fall off. After almost breaking the plate and nearly stabbing myself in the leg I came to realize that I had to be crazy to be doing this. Why was I allowing my insane desire for this food to interfere with my life? Something had to help me.

The seed that OA had planted was sending out shoots. I threw out the rest of the cake and rushed home ready for something, anything. My wife handed me a food plan and told me that it would work only in conjunction with the rest of the program and it would work only if I was completely honest and ready.

Within two weeks, my wife and three other people began an OA meeting in our area. I was losing weight and upon my third week of abstinence I was allowed to lead the meeting.

I have learned in this program why I ate and why I felt as I did about myself. Within the first ten months I lost more than 115 pounds and had begun maintenance. I read all the literature that was available, went to as many meetings as possible (and if there wasn't a meeting, I started one) and gave away my program to as many people as possible. I began to find that meetings just weren't enough. I got involved in forming an intergroup, I began traveling out of my area to go to meetings and marathons. When we felt the need of a step meeting and I didn't know how to go about starting one, I drove more than one hundred miles to go to one so that I could bring it back home. I even went to other states seeking the strength I needed to keep me going.

I recently learned that I can't work the program for anyone but myself. Those who go to meetings have found the program; what they do with it is their business, and I accept them as they are. However, there are thousands who are still locked up in their minds, still eating, suffering and perhaps near death. It is those people who need our help. It is my responsibility, the responsibility of all of us in our Fellowship to find them and tell them that there is a way, that we have found the answer. If the seed does not sprout, give it time.

I was never able to cry in public until someone in the program told me it was OK. Trees need water to grow and so do people; that's why God gave us tears. We must give our brothers and sisters room to grow. I must extend my hand with no conditions, no expectations — only the hope that they will find what I have found.

3

It Wasn't Fair

*I*T JUST WASN'T FAIR. I was sixteen years old and weighed almost 300 pounds. I don't really know how I got there. It was as if I were living in a nightmare for sixteen years and suddenly woke up, fat and afraid. I cried all the time, but could never really explain why. I was tired of diets and sick of trying to lose weight.

My life was given over to food: hiding it, sneaking it, then counting calories and trying every new fad diet that came along. My sole purpose in life seemed to be to lose weight. I would vow to become a certain weight or a certain size before the next school year or the next birthday, only to fail again. That was my life. I was miserable. I still shudder to remember what it was like in those days.

I remember how awful it felt to be the youngest and

fattest wherever I went. In public and at family gatherings, I was acutely conscious of my size and my age. I was always the one with the charming personality.

"If only she would lose weight, she would be adorable," the aunts and other relations would cluck. They never intended to hurt my feelings. But I was very good at hiding my feelings.

Actually, my best friends and strongest supporters were my family and their friends. It seems strange, but the people closest to me were all much older than I. Now I know that it was because I was ridiculed and rejected by my peers. Kids can be so cruel.

I still remember the all-school assembly in sixth grade when I was initiated into safety patrols. Everyone laughed when that fluorescent orange belt wouldn't fit around me. Or the time in the junior high school cafeteria when my classmates threw peanuts at me, and choruses of "Dumbo!" echoed through the lunchroom.

But the most painful time of all was in the tenth grade when the class yearbook came out. There was a full-page picture of me, close to 300 pounds, leaning against a tree. The caption identified me by name, and joked in print that I was "holding up the tree."

But kids aren't the only ones who lack compassion. It took me a long time to ride a bike again after the man who lived around the corner called me over just to say hello, then proceeded to laugh hysterically about the way the bike tires would flatten to the rim every time I sat down.

The utter humiliation of that fat! The first time I ever undressed in the locker room, the other girls laughed and joked and pointed to the rolls and layers of blubber. They thought they were teasing; I'm sure they didn't intend to be so cruel. But I never gave them another chance to hurt me like that. From that day on,

I always wore my gym shorts and T-shirt under my clothes. My school clothes were a uniform, anyway: stretch pants and a knit top. What did it matter if I added another layer? Not many stylish clothes for teenagers come in size 46 and 48. There were no gym suits large enough to fit me, of course, and I never could wear a Girl Scout uniform. I was the only girl in my troop without one. I also was the only student in my high school hospital careers class without the traditional white coat. They didn't have one large enough.

Teachers didn't help, either. It was humiliating enough to have to dress differently from the other kids for gym class, but then the teacher would send me off by myself in an auxiliary gym with nothing to keep me company but a boring "inches off" exercise book. They wouldn't let me participate in games or sports. I guess they thought I might keel over.

Thank God for the few good friends I had during this period. The ones who liked me then, in spite of what I looked like, are the ones I know will always be dear to me.

Although it was food that was making my life so miserable all those years, it always appeared to be my friend. Or so I thought. It kept me company, relieved anxiety and covered up everything I ever felt. Food interfered with living. I can see now I wasn't living, merely existing — and miserably.

It is strange to realize when I look back that I was trying to "get even" with my friends, and especially my family, by eating. How it hurt them to see me eating and apparently not caring what I was doing to myself. I overlooked the fact that although I was hurting them, I was destroying myself.

I hated what I was doing. The games I played for so long were becoming meaningless. I was tired of cleverly devising new ways to cover up what I ate. I had become an expert at eating as much ice cream as possible without letting the bottom of the carton show through. I thought I fooled everyone by not chewing whatever was in my mouth if someone walked into the room unexpectedly.

The only good thing I remember about being fat — at least I considered it positive at the time — was that being obese gave me an unreal sense of power. I was bigger, and my fat made me feel more powerful than my peers. I didn't feel like a girl at all. I had to lose more than a hundred pounds before I felt any sense of femininity. In my fat days I didn't care about my appearance. All I ever wore were big shirts and pants that would stretch, and boys' tennis shoes. I never washed or combed my hair. It's hard to believe I once lived like such a slob, but it's true.

My mother tried to help me. She took me to a popular diet club four different times, the first time when I was only ten years old. I did fairly well on their diet, but I always stopped going after the fifteenth week. I couldn't face that award ceremony which came on the sixteenth week, when you had to walk up in front of a large group of people to receive a pin. I could never bring myself to do that.

When I was thirteen or fourteen, a friend introduced me to another weight-loss group. I was successful there for short periods of time, but I don't remember feeling as if they really cared about me. That was true in the first diet club too.

I guess it was about this same time that the school nurse suggested I visit the public school psychologist. My parents, who all along would have given anything for me to lose weight, agreed I should go. For the next two years I met with a doctor every Wednesday afternoon. I suppose he tried, but he never really understood how I felt. Each counseling session became a contest to see if I could cry louder than he yelled.

"It's not that difficult," he would scream at me. "You just don't give a damn!"

If he only could have known how very much I cared.

I cared enough to try acupuncture next, a drastic step. I was positive this was the answer. I didn't know a whole lot about it, but at that point I was near the end of my rope and so was my family. After a long family discussion about the cost of acupuncture treatment — and some caustic comments about my determination to stick with it — we decided to give it a whirl.

It cost more than $100 to have the staple inserted in my ear, and ten dollars a week for the treatment. But it wasn't long before I simply stopped going. Interestingly enough, the acupuncture treatment worked well physically. It did decrease my appetite. But it did not decrease my intake of food. I ate whether I was hungry or not.

To this day I don't really know why I came to OA. I was sure I was destined to be fat forever. I read about OA in the newspaper, and one Thursday night I made my way to a meeting. I don't know what made me go. I do know I didn't like it. I have no memory of the speaker, topic or discussion. All I saw at that meeting was the tops of my shoes. I never looked up, but tried to hide my tears by hanging my head. I still remember the way the teardrops beaded on the tops of my shoes, never really sinking in. The OA philosophy didn't sink in, either — at least not that night.

It took only about a half hour of that torture for me to decide that OA wasn't for me. I ran from the room, leaving the meeting in the middle of the discussion, wiping my teary eyes and hoping against hope that my mother and sister would come by early to pick me up.

I stood there in the dark by the curb, utterly alone, depressed and feeling that once again a group had failed me. No one cared.

But that's where OA people are different from any I had ever known before. I heard footsteps behind me. I didn't know who it was, but I knew she was from the OA group inside. She didn't know me, had no personal reason for following me outside. She just came to give me a hug, assure me she cared, and hoped I would come back. If she had not made that effort to reach out to me, to take the time to tell me more about the program, I know I would have added OA to my list of failures. I'll always remember what she did for me that night, and I'll always be grateful.

Through that caring person, I found a sponsor, a beautiful person. She not only was — and is — a super sponsor, but our relationship has grown and blossomed into a caring and trusting friendship.

Nobody else would have put up with what I put her through. She never complained. She spent many hours patiently explaining how the program works. My first few weeks in OA were spent on an erratic on-again, off-again abstinence. But that was OK. My sponsor was patient, loving and understanding. I could sense her caring, her willingness to share what I needed. One Thursday night I was talking with her on the phone as usual, only this conversation was different. I broke down, crying my heart out, pouring out my feelings of worthlessness and confusion.

"Stop!" she said suddenly. "We've got to talk. I want you to meet me in front of the church where your OA meeting is."

It was a bitter cold, icy night, and she drove all the way down from the opposite end of the county. I couldn't understand why anyone would come so far on such a night for me, but I went and met her. That was the first time I had met her in person, and that was my first day of abstinence. I have been abstinent ever since, more than a year now. It was through her support, and the help and guidance of many others like her that I have been able to maintain a good, strong, unshakable abstinence — and a weight loss of more than 111 pounds so far.

During my first six months in the program, I felt as if I were being tested over and over again. I refused to go to parties in the beginning because I was afraid I'd lose my abstinence. I couldn't handle the food choices. Eventually, I didn't hurt so much and could handle holidays and family gatherings without overeating, or even being tempted to overeat.

Some of these family occasions seemed interminable. I remember my uncle's birthday party, where I spent half the evening locked in the bathroom with a box of Kleenex and the telephone I had pulled through the door.

How clearly my sponsor spoke to me that night, reminding me of my own responsibility, and assuring me that I was capable of making the right choices. Again that night, she comforted me with those simple words I've heard so often and still need to hear: "It's going to be all right. Just continue to follow the program."

My sponsor never failed me on those occasions when I needed to talk, to be reassured. I called her from parties, from restaurants, from school, from wherever I was, for whatever I needed.

A few weeks after that night came my birthday. I know birthdays are supposed to be happy occasions, but I was new in the program. And I was only seventeen years old. I felt deprived without that traditional birthday cake with candles. It just wasn't fair that I had to give up an old birthday tradition for a new way of life that was not yet comfortable.

How my feelings and my lifestyle changed over the next few months!

One night I was having dinner out with friends when I had one of those insights that come from the OA program. I suddenly realized — for the first time — that I simply couldn't eat the same way as most of my friends. But I didn't resent it or in any way feel deprived. It was just a fact of life.

I excused myself and quickly ran to a public telephone to call my sponsor. She had helped me through so much, patiently talked me through so many bad times, that it was only fair that I also share my growth and joy with her, too.

That night was exciting. I went to sleep feeling on top of the world. So what if I couldn't eat certain foods! I was just beginning to wake up and live in a world that before OA was only a fantasy. Food no longer ruled my life. I was free. I had recently bought my very first pair of pants with pockets and a zipper (instead of an elastic waistband). I had passed my driver's test and had my operator's license. My family and friends were thrilled about my weight loss. People cared about me, and I cared for them. And I honestly cared about myself. I came to understand that if I eat compulsively I'm not being fair to myself.

Then I finally realized that it wasn't life all those years that hadn't been fair to me; it was I who hadn't been fair to myself. That was something I could change, and right then I decided I would.

I did change and grow in lots of ways from that point on. Some changes and growth came unexpectedly and tragically. When I had been in the program less than a year, my mother died suddenly. One day she was there, and the next she wasn't.

The pain was acute, and the wound deep. It took a long time to heal, but food wasn't part of the medication. My Higher Power and my OA friends gave me the strength to work through the grief and survive, a stronger person. I know now that my finding OA when I did was no coincidence, and that my very special sponsor was a gift — the right person in the right place at the right time.

The night before my mother died, she and I had gone to an OA meeting together. I was so proud of her, and I know she was proud of me. I feel great comfort in knowing she died abstinent. I truly believe it was God's way of showing me the importance of OA in my life.

I know that as long as I follow the OA program, everything I must face in life will turn out all right, and my life will be as fair to me as I allow it to be.

4

A Program of Suicide Prevention

I HAVE BEEN A COMPULSIVE overeater all my life. Up until the time when I became responsible for the food that went into my mouth, I suspect that I was fed compulsively.

I come from a typical Jewish family where food was love. I was raised with the concept that a fat child is a happy child. I could never understand why, if that was true, I was always so miserable.

Though I was a fat child and a chubby teenager, it wasn't until my freshman year in college that my disease really began to progress. I was living in the dorms, away from home for the first time, in a competitive college environment and I simply couldn't cope. So I ate. By the end of that year I weighed about 220 pounds.

I went on the then-popular water diet and got down to about 160. This is where my story differs from many

33

I've heard. It was the only time I ever dieted or lost weight. I never tried the shots or pills or this or that diet. I knew I would fail, so why bother? Besides, I was good at being fat. I wore the cutest size 22 clothes, and I always looked happy to other people.

I remember the exact moment when the water diet ended and my disease ran rampant once again. I was living with my parents and was home one night watching television with my father. My father, a very quiet man, was eating a doughnut and I knew I wanted it. I looked at him and said, "If you don't give me that doughnut I'm going to eat your foot."

Naturally, not being one to "deprive" his children, my father gave me the doughnut. That was the beginning of the end for me. I dropped out of college after my freshman year and started working fulltime. I moved out of my parents' home and started hanging out with a group of people who were into drugs and alcohol. I thought that if I did what they did maybe they would like me, and also if I was drunk or loaded the pain and loneliness might go away, even for a little while.

I began a relationship with a homosexual man which was to last five years. We loved each other, in our own sick ways, but I continually put expectations on him that he could not possibly meet. Although he was bisexual, he had a decided preference for men. I complained about how horribly he treated me, but I made no move to end the relationship.

I believe that my compulsive overeating stems in part from my inability to accept my sexuality; I guess I couldn't come up with a better way to cancel myself out as a woman than to weigh 200 pounds and be involved with a gay man. When this relationship finally ended, my life consisted solely of working, sleeping and eating.

The night I went to my first OA meeting, my life

began in a way I never dreamed possible. I knew I was home. I began abstaining that same night, and I have shed 60 pounds. For me, OA is not a program about food. It is a program of suicide prevention. It is not "cool" for a nice Jewish girl to slash her wrists or O.D. on pills, but I could eat myself to death and not be doing anything out of the ordinary or unacceptable to my family and others around me. What a slow and painful death it would have been!

In OA, I felt a love and acceptance that I had never known before even with my own family. My weight loss has made a difference in my life, but not nearly as great a difference as the changes I have made emotionally and spiritually. Today, I am a functioning human being learning how to live in this world one day at a time. I don't have to hide anymore. I can relate to people on an honest level and I can love myself and know that I am loved by others.

Just for today, I have not found it necessary to break my abstinence. OA took away all my excuses, and for that alone I am grateful.

5

Compulsive Like Me

I WAS ONE OF SIX children. My family, of Italian extraction, started out well but the Depression touched our lives as it did so many.

I can remember some very happy times but I also remember never having enough of anything, not even necessities such as food and clothing. Though I was not fat as a child, I could never get my fill of food. Whenever I could, I stole pennies and bought candy or cookies.

When my father became ill we moved from the city to a small community near the ocean. Our new house was built on stilts and stood at the end of a street that backed up to a canal. The canal became a means of survival for the family. We fished, rented rowboats and sold fish door to door. We ate fish two or three times a day. Fried eels was not an unusual breakfast.

Parental discipline was so strict that even as a teen-ager I was not allowed to date or wear makeup. As I began to earn money, I bought junk food and filled up on it before going home to a pot of whatever my mother had cooked, mostly starches. This practice launched me on what I knew was a very selfish, sneaky way to live.

At sixteen, I was five-foot, one-inch tall and a dumpy 128 pounds. When one of my sisters made fun of me, I went on a dill pickle diet to lose weight. I lost the weight, but I became rundown and caught a cold that turned into a severe case of pneumonia.

In the hospital I was so close to death, a priest gave me final rites. In the worst stage of my illness I kept asking for the man I was to marry, whom I had met and fallen in love with when I was fourteen. He came to my bedside with his sister and gave me a friendship ring. I started a great recovery. We dated after that, but only on Sundays, and I had to be home at ten, a curfew my father imposed.

Father was a wine alcoholic and he was usually drunk. Every week he embarrassed me and tormented my mother trying to get her to promise that she would take me for a Monday morning checkup to see if I was still a virgin. She never did. I was twenty years old and a virgin when I was married.

In the next two years, through pregnancy and pounds gained and lost, I tried unsuccessfully to get down to my normal size. There was no doubt now about my compulsion to overeat.

One day, fat and unhappy at 130 pounds, I happened to read a book about the Roman Empire. It told of feasts lasting several days and the beautiful marble basins called vomitoriums where wealthy Romans and their guests induced vomiting in order to be able to continue eating and drinking.

The ugly seed was planted. Not long after reading that book I bought a huge strawberry shortcake. I sat down with a cup of coffee and ate one piece after another until I had finished the cake. Nausea swept over me. I barely made it to the bathroom where the whole cake came up. It was unpleasant, but afterward I felt good. A few days later I repeated the performance.

I regarded this incredible feat as my own secret discovery. It was as though I had a special trick and whenever I felt like eating some food that took my fancy I performed this trick.

The weight fell off. At 110 pounds I felt very comfortable. Now, how does an overeater stay at 110? By eating and throwing up. I did it for nearly thirty years. My wardrobe size never changed. My family and friends marveled at the food I could consume without getting fat. They said, "Isn't she lucky, she can eat anything and everything and not gain a pound." I heard remarks like that all my adult life and I cringed with guilt.

But I had become an accomplished sneak and conniver. Years went by and slim, trim Cora remained the same. At first I binged every couple of months, then monthly, weekly, daily and finally three or four times a day. I couldn't understand why I did it. Each day I made a solemn vow to stop. I must never put my fingers down my throat again, I told myself. But I couldn't stop. I wanted more and more food. Huge quantities of all sorts of food. It got to a point where I didn't choose anything. It just became everything in sight.

My ritual was always the same: I would eat until my stomach hurt. I had to stand very straight in order not to feel the terrible discomfort. Then I would run to the bathroom and turn on the tap so no one would hear me. I always washed my hands because I didn't want a disease in my mouth. The disease that was in my head raged unchecked.

Years passed and I saw my own daughter and my sisters getting fat. Many times it occurred to me to tell them my secret, but I was ashamed. In thirty years I never broke my silence.

When my sister began attending OA meetings, she sent literature about the program to my daughter who by now weighed more than 200 pounds. I had been praying for her, not yet aware of how sick I was. But I was close to the bottom of the pit. I wanted to stop. Each time I looked into the toilet bowl, fear gripped me. I thought, someday I am going to die right here locked in the bathroom. Alone.

One day, I could not vomit. The muscles in my throat refused to work. I kept trying, defiant and full of fear at the same time.

"Oh my God," I thought. "I've done it. I ruined my throat." The next day I was so nervous and afraid, I didn't eat. My dilemma was indescribable.

At this point my daughter, who was now in OA, opened a door that was to show me the way out. She invited me to go to a meeting so I could meet her friends. I went and I listened. I bought some literature and I started my secret OA. I cold turkeyed alone. How could I ask anyone to sponsor me? Overeaters were fat; I was thin.

I took God as my sponsor. Each day I said the Serenity Prayer. I did not know how much I could eat and not gain weight. But I had stopped putting my fingers down my throat. Joyfully, through this program and God's grace, I have just celebrated four years of freedom from that obsession.

After one and a half years of working the program alone, I was still afraid. My weight was slowly creeping up. I reached 124 pounds. Here was another turning point, a new decision to be faced: throw up or get fat —

or come out of the closet.

I chose to live. I chose OA. I humbled myself and walked into a room full of overweight people. They stared at me. But I needed them. I took a sponsor and began abstinence, which I have had one day at a time for the past two and a half years.

What a joy to get on the scale once a week and find my weight 107 or 108 pounds! It has been a beautiful four years. At first, weight loss was my goal. After reaching it I chose two new goals. One is to grow emotionally and the other, spiritually. It hasn't been an easy road. After years of giving my life nothing but guilt, misery, fear, depression and no self-worth, I have had restored to me the soundness of mind and body that was God's gift to me at birth.

How blessed I feel that the people in OA didn't judge me as different, but understood that I have the same food compulsion they have. Their acceptance opened the doors to so much for me. I have learned how to be honest. My first amends were to my daughter. I told her everything, and from that moment on I felt I wasn't alone anymore. It embarrasses her to hear that she saved my life, but it's true.

Finally, I told my husband. I had been hiding literature and going to meetings secretly. He was shocked. But I went on to ask his pardon for all the food money I stole and for the lavish meals I let him buy me only to feed my obsession.

Now I have a new peace. I had been a human ship, tossing about in life, looking for a port — and at last I found one. OA is my resting place, my comfort, my serenity and joy. I shall never, and can never go back to that stormy sea of food obsession.

6

Crisis Center Volunteer

*T*HE MIRACLE IN my life began just five years ago when I overheard someone mention Overeaters Anonymous. I laughed nervously and said, "What is that?" My friend told me and as I stood in front of her, some 60 pounds overweight, I said, "I think I need that. Where is it?"

Three days later I attended my first meeting, and a month after that I left OA in confusion. I was an unhappy, guilt-ridden, indecisive, bossy, much-fragmented person who thought I had it all together because I managed to fool so many other people into believing it.

I was a volunteer at the Crisis Center, talking to people who were suicidal. One day a woman who weighed 300 pounds called, and guess who took that call? Do you think the Higher Power had anything to do with that? Here I was, talking to suicidal people, a 200-pounder trying to help a 300-pounder.

That day I quit the Crisis Center and began to take my own crisis seriously enough to do something about it. I reached out to OA once again. This time I was desperate enough to stay, ask questions and really listen. I found that these people shared my pain, anxiety, loneliness, despair and unquenchable appetite for what I thought was food. I stayed to learn that my hunger was spiritual and that what I was searching for could not be found in food. These OA members were not strangers, even though I did not know them nor was I to know any of their last names for a long time.

I remember well the day I received the gift of abstinence: October 10, my youngest daughter's birthday. She was seventeen years old and, like any good mom, I baked a cake. Of course, I was not going to eat any, but as I gazed at the thing I felt sorry for poor me and said, half aloud, "If I cannot ever eat that again I don't know if I want to live."

I am glad I said it aloud because my words shocked me. I remembered my mother often saying to us children, when we ate too much, "Do you live to eat or do you eat to live?" I realized that I still thought it preferable to live to eat. Then and there, I understood that food was my false idol. I put it before everything.

I went to the kitchen window and gazed outside at the trees and flowers and the sun shining brightly. I prayed to God not to let food be my life, my false idol any longer. My prayer was answered that day. The pounds began to melt off.

That spring, my husband of twenty-five years and I went away together to learn more about ourselves and how to talk with one another and love each other better. In the fall, I signed up to take a class at the local community college, something which I had wanted to do for years. Funny, isn't it, that I could be a volunteer for a Crisis Center and too fearful to go back to school.

The day before my first class was to begin, we received word that our oldest son, Bill, had been killed in a car accident. I missed my first class, but went to the second one a week later. Something in me knew that if I didn't go to school that day I never would.

After our son died, people brought in food — mounds of it, and most of it fattening. I knew I couldn't turn to food now or I would never find my way out of despair. I asked a close OA friend to choose the food for me to eat at this time. It was the only way I could make it.

I continued school, taking carefully chosen classes. A paper I wrote for my English class not only got an A+ but it won a contest. It was a story about my mother-in-law and writing it helped me in making amends. It made her very proud and happy, and I won first prize — a hundred dollars. I even had my picture in the paper, and it was a thin picture!

The summer after I lost my excess weight I went camping, backpacking and hiking up into the Sierras with my family and some friends. It was the first such adventure of my whole life. I had always stayed home when my family went backpacking. Being so overweight, I couldn't have managed another heavy pack. Even thin, it was hard. It was nine and a half miles up and down a difficult trail. But I made it. I had a headache for two hours afterward, but as I lay on the hard ground I was exultant.

The top of a mountain seems to sharpen the senses. I saw the beautiful wildflowers — pinks, yellows, purples, blues. The stars were closer than I had ever seen them.

I am delighted to say that I haven't missed a camping trip since that first year. I don't even get a headache anymore.

7

The Great American Wife

*M*Y MOTHER PREPARED me well for the role of fat person. Being overweight herself (as a child I thought my mother was the fattest person in the world), she knew well how my life would run.

She told me how people treated you: the jokes, the rejections, the cruelty. What Mother stressed was that it didn't matter. It wasn't what you looked like that counted, it was what you were inside.

"Develop your mind," she told me. "That's something they can never take away from you."

I got the idea that all that mattered was whether you were happy or not. You only had one life and if you didn't enjoy it, it was wasted. Why deprive yourself and be slim? Soon you'd be dead and it wouldn't matter anyway. You could have enjoyed life, but you didn't.

Other people just didn't understand. Already, "they"

were on one side and I was on the other. And that was how I found the world to be. I never quite fit in. I was always scared, or awkward, or superior. But different; always different.

Mother was a good cook and set a good table. We had garden fresh vegetables, plenty of meat and several desserts at each meal every day. Chubby was healthy and eating was pleasing your folks. Cooking showed love.

Love wasn't expressed otherwise. It was an embarrassing subject. No one touched or hugged. You knew they loved you. There was no need to get mushy about it.

If you had a headache or a cold, special foods were prepared. And if you had a fever or had to go to the doctor, nothing was too much trouble. They'd go to the store and get anything. Eating made you feel better.

On your birthday you got to dictate the family menu. Dining out was a super-special occasion. Holidays were times when the whole family gathered at our house and the food preparations went on for days. Even minor events turned out to be feasts.

The way the family felt about food made it seem natural to eat when I felt good and when I felt bad.

The foods I loved were potatoes, breads, beans and sweets — no salads, no vegetables. Other kids might lick the pan when their mom baked a cake; I licked the pan when Mother made creamed potatoes.

I made good grades in school and was an honor student. This won me approval at home and with my teachers. I soon found a kind of belonging by appeasing authority figures, and it became a way of life. This was easy because you didn't have to obey all the rules. All you had to do was be "sweet" and give the appearance of doing as you were told. Being sneaky turned out to be one of my great natural talents. It also compensated for not fitting in with the kids. I told myself that I was above the rank and file, smarter. I wasn't interested in silly, girly things like clothes, makeup and boys. Even school functions such as ballgames and carnivals were too childish for me.

Things changed at home, though, once I got into high school. Not the cooking — all the great stuff was still piled high. But suddenly I was supposed to "care more about yourself than that." Mother started picking at me constantly about what I ate and how much I ate. Boys weren't going to have anything to do with me if I kept on.

So that became my goal in life: to get married and be the great American wife and mother. If being happy was what mattered, that was what it was going to take to make me happy.

I got married the day after I graduated from high school. My life was planned. My ideals were set. I believed in control. You had to control your life and make it exactly as you wanted it to be because it was the only one you had.

When I was growing up, my grandmother lived with us and I saw the conflicts and tensions brought about by that situation. I promised myself I would never let that happen to me and ruin my life. No parents, his or mine, would ever live with us.

Also, I would never work. I believed in the sanctity of the home. I had my role to live.

To obtain the things I wanted, no price was too high to pay. I knew only too well that I was not sexually attractive. But I was willing to make up for that in other ways. I waited on my new husband hand and foot. I pandered to his ego, gave in to him on every decision, large and small. He got my total respect and dedication.

In return I wanted protection — insulation from the

world. My home was going to provide that.

I didn't fit into my wife role any better than I had fit into school. I had nothing in common with other young wives. I stayed home and got bored and depressed. I ate.

No babies came. We were the only couple around with no children. I thought it was cruel. I hated being around anyone else; all they talked about was babies.

I gained weight slowly, eight or nine pounds each year. At first, because I didn't have anything else to do, I put a lot of time and thought into special recipes. Supper became a grand occasion. Later it relieved tensions.

Being compliant caused problems. I handled the money and if my husband asked if we could afford to go somewhere or buy something, I couldn't say no. I felt guilty, both because I knew I should be managing the money better and because most other young wives were working to help out, especially those with no children at home.

We got behind on some of our bills. We went into debt over our heads, unable to control our charge account buying. If we wanted something, we got it.

I could not stand to be a failure at managing money, so now I lied to my husband about paying the bills and neglected to mention dodging the bill collectors. My old ally, sneakiness, came to the rescue again.

There is only one thing wrong with that kind of dishonesty. Sometimes you don't feel real. Someone can tell you he loves you, and you say to yourself, "Yes, you think that. But if you really knew me — how I am inside — you wouldn't love me at all."

So you come to understand that your whole life is built on a pretty shaky foundation. It's scary at times. But you go on.

I became bitter. I was smarter than this. Things

should turn out better. It wasn't my fault that we didn't have children. That was a dirty trick being played on me.

Some things I could control, though. If we didn't have enough money, there were ways of stretching it a bit. If life wouldn't give me a fair share, then I'd take it. There are ways of beating the system, of outsmarting "them."

That was when the shoplifting began, and it was emotional dynamite right from the start. Like the rest of my life, the stealing soon became focused on food. It was almost as though someone else was doing it, not me. Not once did I consider myself a thief. I was just trying to cope.

Things weren't right. The happiness was not coming. My husband insisted I get out of the house and get a job. Both for myself and to alleviate our financial situation. I did, and I hated him for it.

Fear was growing, and my body along with it as I ate more. What I had believed in turned out to mean nothing. So now I believed in nothing.

Then, life dealt me the crushing blow: it became necessary to move my husband's mother into our home. I would not accept it. My stealing increased. I began having violent headaches, almost constantly. And I became a sneak eater. I nibbled while I cooked, then ate a large meal and finally I cleaned off all the plates and finished whatever was left in the serving bowls. After that, I tucked several slices of lunchmeat into the pocket of my robe and went into the bathroom.

My desk drawer at work always had three or four candy bars in it. I ate in the car. I ate in the middle of the night. At five feet in height, I weighed 232 pounds and was getting heavier. I couldn't tie my shoelaces. My feet swelled and my legs ached; I had to buy ankle braces, and even then the veins in my feet looked as though they were about to burst.

At this point my mother, who was in her forties, had a heart attack. During the next six years, she had eight heart attacks and three strokes. That mind which she had said they could never take away from you was never quite the same.

Life had no point. I seemed to have no future to look forward to at all. I was sliding downhill with nothing to hold onto. Pain and death lay ahead. And the best of my life lay behind.

Then I saw the ad in the paper for Overeaters Anonymous. I cut out the address and time of the meeting and put it in a kitchen drawer and left it there for four months.

But the ad said help was available and that came back into my head. I still had doubts. A fat club was insulting. And I knew I wouldn't mesh well with other people.

Also, if I tried and failed, which was the result I expected, I didn't want other people to know. I knew they "shared" and all I could equate that with was my Baptist upbringing and the revival testimonials. To that, I had to say, "No way. Definitely not my style."

Still, I went. There wasn't any answer for me anywhere else.

They had me pegged. I knew I was home. I went on the program the next day at 220 pounds.

I would like to be able to say that once I found this program all my problems vanished and I have had perfect abstinence and life has been wonderful. But that has not been my experience.

I wanted the program and I knew it was right for me. But at times I've wanted it my way — and this is one program you don't manipulate. You give it up or you don't.

So my experience has been up and down. Always

growing. Sometimes it's easy; I'm like a kite in the breeze. Sometimes I take it back and resist. Then I bog down and sometimes I break abstinence. But I just go back on.

I would like to be perfect, but I'm not. And there's room here for mistakes. I accept what I can and wrestle with the rest. It's OK.

It has been a year now. I've lost 80 pounds. Ten inches off my bust and ten off my hips. Twelve off my waist. Instead of a 24½ dress I wear a 13.

I am changing, and at times that scares me. I have to keep reminding myself that I'm still me — and always will be. In fact, I am finding the real me for the first time in my life.

I'm less defensive; I don't have to apologize for me. I'm working on me.

Never before did I have enough. Enough love, enough food, enough possessions. I always had to grab. I always felt desperate. Now I am beginning to relax, to feel satisfied.

And for the first time ever, I'm beginning to have a clean, honest feeling inside. I go to bed at night with nothing to hide.

I'm more apt to tell you how I really feel. And I'm less willing to go that extra mile just to make up for being less a person than you.

I'm aware of how sick I've been, of how far I have to go. But that's OK. I know the way.

I wake up in the morning glad to be alive. Life is a good thing.

I have OA, and my life is never going to be the same because of it.

And I have reached my goal: not my desired weight (I still plan to lose 30 pounds), but the only goal that really matters, remember?

I'm happy.

8

The Dancer

*F*ROM THE START I was fighting mad at life and at my parents. It was a constant battle of their will versus mine, and I hated them for being right. But underneath the hate, I loved them.

My food problem, which reflected my approach to life, started early. My weight was not affected, however, because I was very active.

At six, I worshipped the dance teacher next door. She had a gorgeous figure and I wanted to grow up to have a body like hers. My mother suggested that I take lessons, and thus began my career as a dancer. My life was soon entirely dedicated to dancing. I was either taking lessons, teaching or performing. The best part of appearing in shows was the free food afterward. And all I really cared about after a day of teaching was getting to the candy machine and the fast-food stores.

I felt tired and lazy most of the time. I practiced grudgingly, only because my mother insisted that if I wanted to be a good dancer I would have to work at it. I began taking my mother's diet pills and loved feeling alert and energetic. I counted calories, weighed myself obsessively every day and became very thin.

After graduating from high school, I left home to dance at state fairs with a tour group. I finally had time and money to do as I wanted, but all I wanted to do was eat and sleep. I wound up breaking my diet every day. Having convinced myself that I felt superior to the other dancers, I was quite happy to be alone with my food. The diet pills kept me on a superficial high during working hours, but by the end of the summer they were losing their effectiveness. I gained 25 pounds. My costumes were splitting and the boss was about to fire me.

I found stronger diet pills and got my figure back, then entered the "Miss Dance of America" contest. I scored highest in my performance, but I was so nervous I flubbed my interview with the judges and was awarded runner-up instead of the title.

New York City was the place to be to pursue my career so I moved there. In the next few years I had one job after another, coming close to getting fired from each one on account of gaining weight and being habitually late.

One night I came face to face with the real nature of my sickness. At four in the morning I threw a coat over my nightgown and raced to an all-night food store where I talked them into letting me take the food on credit. Returning to my apartment, I started shaking in the elevator, unable to wait. I ripped open the carton of ice cream and began digging into it with my teeth like an animal. Nothing mattered but to eat as much as I could as fast as possible. I didn't even feel guilty, just void of thought.

Finally, it seemed to be over. I was nauseated, disgusted and so numb that I didn't care. But the obsession came back. I had to give in just to get through the night. I returned to the store and again I couldn't eat the stuff fast enough. At last, I fell into a drugged stupor and slept for about twelve hours. I woke up with a confused silence in my mind, bewildered and afraid.

I had a bloated hangover — my face was puffed up and I felt ugly and ashamed. I knew I was like an alcoholic or an addict with food but I didn't know what to do except to start another diet. I cleaned up, took a diet pill and felt hope slowly coming back. "Binging is not where it's at," I observed to myself. "It's definitely a nowhere road."

I wound up binging the whole day.

There were many nights like that. When I grew noticeably fat, the director threatened to fire me if I didn't lose weight. In a panic, I vowed never to do it again. But the conflict was too great. Each time, my weight went a little higher. Between jobs, it soared.

I had developed the art of people pleasing and got along with almost everyone (except bosses) in a surface way, but I felt that something was very wrong underneath. Whenever I visited my family we had screaming arguments. They couldn't understand how anyone in New York could like me. It was as if I were two different people.

My involvements with the opposite sex were as messed up as the rest of my life. I had one bad love affair after another, pushing relationships to an end or becoming overly dependent. Either way, I ended up alone with my food.

I quit using amphetamines after my last show business job and gained 60 pounds. I tried every new diet I could find, went to hypnotists, psychiatrists and a fast-

ing farm, but nothing could stop me. When I saw
people I knew on the street, I hid in shame. I became
almost violent if my parents or others who loved me
tried to help. I hated myself and wished I would die. I
couldn't understand what other people saw in life.
What made them want to get up in the morning? What
motivated them?

My parents told me about a television program on
Overeaters Anonymous. It sounded good, but I didn't
want the answer to come from my parents. I was en-
rolled in a commercial diet club (for the third time)
and insisted it was going to work.

After a week on the diet club regimen, I started binging. Finally, I gave up and went to an OA meeting. From
the start, I knew that this was the answer for me. It was
different from a diet club. Weight was not the main is-
sue. They were talking about a whole way of approaching life. They also kept mentioning God and a Higher
Power, which turned me off, though I tried to be open to
the idea. I had never believed in God — or in anything.
I began to see that this was my problem.

It seemed impossible to stay abstinent. I hated to tell
my sponsor that I had done it again, but I forced myself to be honest. The binging went on for eight
months. Then one day, the latest "new beginning"
turned out to be the last one. I have abstained, one day
at a time, ever since. It has been four and a half years,
and it is still a precious miracle to me that I can enjoy
my food without eating or craving more.

I believe that my abstinence is a gift which I finally
became ready to accept and appreciate — a gift I am
willing to go to any lengths to keep. The program has
shown me what to do to avoid a binge. Just for this one
day I can do it, with help. I have lost 60 pounds, but I
believe I am just as capable of slipping now as ever, so I
try to stay grateful and to develop my dependence on

God instead of food.

Without the food to hide behind, I began to see how afraid I was of life and people. But when I reached out, people were there for me, giving me loving support instead of rejecting me. It has been a steady process of deepening trust and of growing to love myself and others, even with defects.

I did not return to show business after I began abstinence. I chose, instead, to join the business world. During the first two years, I came close to being fired because of the negativity and anger which I could no longer suppress with food. But working the OA program has changed my personality and attitudes. Now I enjoy being responsible and trustworthy. Small accomplishments such as getting to work on time make me feel good.

For a while, my life was built completely around OA and my job. I still attend meetings and sponsor people, but I have gradually opened up to other activities. I have begun developing friendships with men based on honesty rather than fantasies and games. Even my relationship with my parents is improving. I recently tried skydiving, which I would never have considered before OA. Throwing myself out into the sky for all I was worth was the ultimate moment of trust in God and myself!

I never knew life could be like this. I have no idea where it will lead except that, if I stay abstinent, it will be in a positive direction. None of this would have happened if I had given up during those first months of OA when I was still binging. The most important thing I heard in those meetings was, "Keep coming back!" Thank God I did.

9

Rosy Dreams

I DON'T KNOW WHEN I first started escaping into food. I remember blowing my allowance each week at the candy store on the way to school and hitting the cookie jar when I came home to an empty house as early as the second grade.

I was not popular at school. I knew it was because I was fat, headstrong, outspoken, self-centered and inconsiderate. I knew I was all these things: my mother told me often enough.

When I was lonely, food was my friend. It soothed and comforted me and filled the hole that was there when I felt unloved, which was most of the time.

Notice I said "when I felt unloved," not that I was unloved. It was many years, many pounds gained, lost and regained, many men — including a couple of husbands — before I was to begin to learn the difference.

I left home when I was barely seventeen after a blowup with my father. I felt he had turned on me and that without him on my side, life at home would be intolerable.

So began my long search for emotional security. If only I could find someone to love me, life would be beautiful.

I had discovered alcohol during my senior year in high school. Miraculously, the weight came off. I made friends; I even dated a little. For the first time in my life I experienced a sense of belonging.

At eighteen I joined the Air Force. My consumption of alcohol, which had been negligible, hit what was for me an alltime high. I never liked feeling drunk and out of control, yet I would chug-a-lug beer or down double shots of whiskey until I began to feel the effect. Then I would head for the food to sober up before going to bed. Eventually I eliminated the "middleman." Food gave me what alcohol could not: a sense of being satiated yet still "in control."

I thought being married would be a guarantee against loneliness, so at nineteen I married the first man who would have me. By the time our daughter was born a year and a half later, I weighed 178 pounds. All my rosy dreams had been shattered and I was miserable.

The next six years were filled with self-doubt. First my mother and now my husband told me how inadequate and difficult to live with I was.

Through great determination and strenuous effort I lost weight and when my second child, a boy, was seventeen months old, I left my husband.

Soon the old doubts and fears returned and with them all my lost weight. I was alone and desperate in a strange city, with no job, no friends and two small children to support.

Day after day I answered ads with the same result: nothing. I was too big to fit into a waitress uniform, my typing was poor and no one wanted an elephant for a receptionist.

Pressed to lose weight, I joined a health spa, only to give it up as hopeless two weeks later. I was tired of fighting; I finally accepted myself as I was — fat.

A few days later I read an article about Overeaters Anonymous. I went to a meeting, not with hope for myself, but for my daughter who was clearly following in my footsteps.

That was almost three years ago. Through the fellowship of OA and constant effort in working the twelve steps of our program, I have begun to accept and care for myself. With this has come the ability to love others unconditionally.

A short time ago I became aware that I have always been so preoccupied with my need for my mother's acceptance that I never once thought of her need to be accepted by me. When I made an effort to change, our relationship improved dramatically.

I often have relapses into the kind of thinking that would have me believe I need one special person to love and accept me all the time. I still have times of fear and loneliness, but they are shorter and less frequent now. Instead of allowing them to last days or weeks, I find that I am able to reach out to someone almost immediately. When these feelings trigger an emotional "binge" I have been able to stop short and take an honest look at myself.

Today I am maintaining a weight loss of 75 pounds, and I have found within me a Power that can do for me what I could never do for myself.

10

The Search for Love

*A*T THE AGE OF ELEVEN I seemed to recover from a sickly early childhood. I began to "bust out" all over. Coming back from the nurse's office when I was in the fifth grade, everybody wanted to know how much I weighed. That meant I was a fat kid.

I was ugly, too, because in those days girls with long hair were considered old-fashioned. The girls with short hair were the beautiful ones and of course my mother and dad wouldn't cut my hair. It was too long and beautiful and heavy and wavy. But I cried until I finally got my way. When my dad took me to the barbershop and the barber cut my hair there were tears in Dad's eyes.

But the haircut didn't make me attractive because I was wearing size 18 clothes. Can you imagine that on a four-foot, ten-inch kid? I never did get to be very tall, but I grew very wide — almost as wide as I was tall.

Jean Harlow was the idol of the day and I believed that someday I would be beautiful like her. I would be thin, too, because I would go on a magic diet that would be easy to follow and I would have a beautiful figure.

Things didn't work out quite that way. When I became sixteen my mother had a nervous breakdown and it was unbearable in the house with just my dad around. It was during Depression and he didn't work much.

I was not allowed to date so I sneaked out. My first "steady" had a brand new car, and I thought he must be a bootlegger because they were the only people who had any money in those days. I knew because my own parents made and sold wine and beer until my mom was arrested for selling it. We always had beer and wine around the house. My parents drank moderately and only with meals, but my older brother and I found our home brew very pleasant in the evening. We didn't have any soda or other beverage except well water, so we drank beer or wine.

The man I began dating at sixteen drank whiskey. He brought it with him when we went out in his eight-cylinder Oldsmobile. I loved riding in that car, and I liked going to the movies. So when he threatened to stop dating me unless I "proved" I loved him, I gave in. But I didn't love him. Not even when I had to marry him.

In my mother-in-law's house, where we went to live, I began drinking heavily. Everyone else drank. I suspected that both my husband and his mother, as well as the man she lived with, were alcoholics.

That was my life at sixteen. I was fat and I was an alcoholic; and I had a miscarriage.

During the war years, I went to work in a steel mill.

That's where I found out about diet pills. It was the magic way to go.

When I became pregnant again, I became angry. I did not want a baby. I had divorced my husband once, but my brother had persuaded me to go back to him. After our little girl was born, I went back to the diet pills. It was the only way I could keep my figure — not as slim as it should have been, but still not too bad.

When we moved to a new house, we took in roomers. One young man caught my interest and I told him he had to go. My husband was very jealous.

In my third pregnancy, I gained 50 pounds and I nearly died during the delivery. After my recovery, things did not go well at home. My husband and I began drinking more, sometimes to the point of battling with our fists and throwing things at each other. We really got cut up. But I wasn't going to take his battering; I was going to fight back, even if it killed me.

I began counseling, which was to last for years. I didn't tell my counselor much about my drinking and blackouts, but she once told me that an alcoholic is not a person who is down in the gutter but a person who needs alcohol in order to function. That was me, all right. Between eating and drinking I was one sad sack. I had heard of Alcoholics Anonymous, but that was not for me — it was for the drunken slob in the gutter.

Shortly after our son was born, I wrote a Christmas note to the last roomer we had, telling him we had a little boy now and inviting him to drop in and see the baby. He moved back in with us, and he made himself very useful. He could diaper the baby and do all sorts of things around the house. He took over and my husband let him. My husband was lazy. Stamp and coin collecting and watching television were his idea of recreation. He wasn't interested in mowing the lawn or feeding or changing the baby — and after all, Art was dependable, Art was around all the time. He liked Art.

Well, you guessed it. I began to think, why do I need a husband? I needed Art. I could feel the attraction between us growing. And one day in May I found myself in his arms. I knew he wouldn't move out; I didn't want him to.

After four years of counseling, I asked my husband for a divorce. He refused. For one whole year we fought in court. And I drank. At last, the divorce was final and Art and I slipped quietly over the state line and were married. "Now I have heaven on earth," I thought, "My diet pills to keep me thin, my liquor to keep me happy and a husband I love." But something was wrong. We were both drinking. I knew that marriage number two was going to break up.

In late November that year, Art told me he was taking his Christmas vacation. He packed and said, "When I come back, I'm not guaranteeing you that I'm coming here to live. I may get another room somewhere."

After he left and the children were in school, I lay on my bed and said, "Oh God, if you're for real and you can hear me, please change me, because I can't change myself."

About a week later, my husband came home. I stopped drinking.

That was my introduction to the twelve steps. I had hit bottom, found my Higher Power and turned my will and my life over to the care of God. I knew now that AA was where I belonged. I have been sober twenty-one years and ten and a half months.

When I found out that OA was like AA and used the same twelve steps, I sent for a beginner's kit. There were no meetings in our area, so I asked God for three things: that I would lose my weight; that I would find a place for a meeting near a highway; and that people would come.

I lost all my weight while waiting for the beginner's kit and looking for a meeting place. I found one within a mile of not one but five highways. From our first meeting, OA in this area has grown to sixteen groups. I am the outgoing chairman of our intergroup, now leaving my beautiful groups behind and moving to another city. I learned that there are several OA members waiting there to take me to meetings.

What a beautiful thing it is to know that OA has so much love in it for people who really want the recovery. Back in the Thirties I wore a size 18 dress. With diet pills, I managed to go down to an 11. Now, through OA, I have been maintaining a weight loss of about 40 pounds for four and a half years. And I now wear a size 3 dress.

11

Sink the Lollipop!

*I*N A FAMILY OF TEN children, I was number nine and the only girl. My father left us when I was a year old, and my brothers, never short of playmates, did not deign to play with a girl. At the age of eleven, I was sexually molested.

It does not seem far-fetched to suspect that these experiences made me wary of the male sex. Now in my fifties, I feel I have not been able to trust men enough to want one for a husband. Boyfriends I have had; a permanent relationship, never.

It was well before I entered my teens that I began to build my ship. I made it out of pure chocolate, and it was my sanctuary for thirty-nine years. Aboard my ship, I worked my way up to ten to twenty candy bars a day plus a variety of other chocolate concoctions. By the age of sixteen I had reached 240 pounds.

Within the huge body was an emotionally contorted child. When things got out of hand, as they usually did, I expected people to look after me. I grew angry with God when He would not do as I wished and turned to the medical profession, demanding that doctors do for me what God wouldn't.

I set impossible goals for myself and became angry when I didn't reach them. But candy solved all my problems. It relieved depressions, eliminated the need to make decisions and was a handy, all-purpose reward, as appropriate for failure as for success.

Many times I ventured out of my magic ship, vowing never to return. But I always did. I was safe there and no one else could come aboard to criticize me. During my brief absences I visited many doctors. They all said the same thing, "Lose weight or else." I did; in fact, I went up and down as regularly as the waves in the ocean. It began to be clear to me that death was not going to wait until I grew old to claim me. But I really didn't care. I had decided by this time that I would die on my ship and die happy. I did not realize how long it takes or how painful it would be.

When I contracted rheumatoid arthritis at the age of thirty, the doctor asked me, "Have you gone through an emotional crisis recently?"

"My whole life has been an emotional crisis," I replied.

My condition of psychic chaos was on slow simmer until one June day when I was told that I would die if I didn't lose weight. (As if I didn't know.) I was also informed that there was now a way to lose weight which didn't require willpower. It was a surgical procedure called the intestinal bypass. Out of everything the doctor said, I heard only "You can eat and still lose weight" and "You will have a lot of diarrhea."

I waited until my weight reached 308 pounds and

then submitted to the operation. Thus began eight years of hell. The lowest point my weight reached after the bypass was 240 pounds. Then it began to yo-yo. I had diarrhea so badly I could not leave the house for a whole year. I finally got so I could control this condition somewhat, and then the flatulence started. It was very degrading.

After three years, I started having kidney trouble. I underwent two operations for the removal of stones and then a third to remove a kidney. That was the beginning of a five-year ordeal during which I had twenty-five operations, eleven related to the damaged kidney.

I suffered acute attacks of pain which the doctors could not explain. I had rashes and allergies. I was extremely short-winded and could hardly move about. The only social life I had was visiting doctors and, occasionally, my family.

Three days after my kidney was removed the doctors told me I had to have the bypass reversed or I would develop trouble with the other kidney, in which case I would have less than three years to live. I decided at this point that it was too painful to die. Still, I could not give up my only solace. I retreated to my ship. I ate because I was sick and I was sick because I ate.

Eight years after the bypass was performed, it was reversed with the warning that I had no chance of pulling through. But again I was saved, though it seemed to me that death would have been better. I felt only pain. Nothing else. Now I was convinced that I had lost my last chance of ever being thin. I had tried everything and there was absolutely nowhere else to go.

As if on cue, the incision opened up and became infected. It drained for four months. The doctors gave up and said it would drain the rest of my life.

It was imperative now to blot out my situation. My

weight climbed back up to 291 pounds. Suddenly, I became aware of what I was doing. I knew I did not want to reach the 300-pound mark again. For the first time I said, "God, help me!"

On Valentine's Day I received what I had asked for in the form of a telephone number a friend had given me more than two years earlier. I had put it in a drawer and forgotten it. I called the number and on the day of love I hobbled into my first OA meeting. I could hardly walk across the room. I was told later that they didn't know if they were going to have to carry me out after the meeting. I was a mess physically and emotionally.

But at that very first meeting I saw a ray of hope. I went to another meeting the next night and I started abstaining the following day. On that day, the incision which the doctors said would drain the rest of my life stopped draining and began to heal.

Out of the total desperation in which I came, I was willing to accept anything OA had to offer. I did not understand much of what was going on, but I knew I wanted what I saw. I started the program by doing everything I was supposed to do: abstaining, speaking, volunteering for service, writing and giving away my inventory, becoming a sponsor. I went to as many meetings as possible and worked the steps to the best of my ability. It took me four months to begin to understand what I was doing.

I had felt for years that I had lost my faith. I could not ask God for anything because He never heard me. Then one night I was told, "Action is the magic word," and I found that I had not lost my faith. It had been there all the time, waiting for me to start acting on it. Once I started the action, things got better. Now I am learning to take responsibility for myself. I have found a small part of me. I know I am a human being and a child of God. That is a wonderful thing to know. It's so much better than being a "freak of nature." I am aware that my life was an emotional crisis because I let it be.

My physical problems are beginning to disappear. I grow stronger every day. I now sail into meetings (I leave my cane at home). At one meeting I climb two flights of stairs. I read all the literature I can get my hands on and enjoy every word. I let my Higher Power run my life and, friends, you cannot believe the things I accomplish in twenty-four hours. I visit people in the hospital, write, read, call OA friends and always have time to talk to them if they call me. All this from a person who, less than two months before coming to OA, spent Christmas in a wheelchair.

It's a beautiful life this Higher Power has created for us, and I for one really want to live and enjoy it.

Off in the distance sits that chocolate ship of mine. I do not have to go back to it unless I choose to. Thank God, today I have a choice.

Stick around, folks. I am going to sink the Good Ship Lollipop.

12

He Just Needed a Diet

*F*IVE YEARS — I figured I had five years left. Lisa would be ten and . . . It was a macabre kind of quietus to make. But at 400 pounds, one has to deal with the essentials.

My wife has admitted that she used to plan what she would do if she awakened to find me dead beside her. "I would simply close the doors, send the children across the street to a neighbor and make arrangements to get what was left of you out of the house quickly."

It was all because that pizzeria had opened so close to home. And the fact that supermarkets were open twenty-four hours, and I was such a terrible sleeper. One thing for sure, it had nothing really to do with what was going on inside of me; that much I was sure of. I was "the most happy fella."

I grew up in a family of happy people. Everyone

compulsively ate, compulsively vied for center stage and compulsively outshouted, outtalked and outraged each other. (I remember a thin cousin from New Jersey whom we saw infrequently. She just never seemed to fit in.) My world within these parameters was secure and unflawed.

When I first attended elementary school, I was chagrined at the number of "thinnies" who were there. I firmly believed what my mother had told me. "Thin people, they're not well." They — nearly my entire school — were short-timers. I was afraid to make friends for fear I'd lose them to their disease, or whatever it was that caused thinness.

I remember once asking a friend if he ever slept on his mother's arm. He looked at me askance. "Sure," he replied as I stared at his fashionably shaped mother. Such thin arms. I thought of how I "fluffed" my mother's arm like a pillow until it just fit. I truly pitied my friends and their thin mothers.

I knew after my grade school weigh-in (I found myself double everyone else's weight), that it was I who was different. Final confirmation came from Mom. I was invited to dinner at a friend's house. She took me aside and explained.

"Other people do not eat like we do. Remember not to embarrass Momma. If you watch yourself, Momma will put something aside for you on the stove. It'll be your favorite!"

I was electrified. During dinner at my friend's I spoke intermittently. I was transfixed with the idea that something "special" was waiting for me. I needed to get home to it.

"You've eaten so little," my friend's mother noted.

"I never eat," I retorted.

"But . . ." It was accompanied by a sidelong glance.

"My mother says I'm glandular."

I ran home that evening and many others to the starchy promise awaiting me on the stove. All my life, whenever I ate out, I had a homing response. My wife often remarked that I always needed a fourth meal when I ate out anywhere. It was ancient programming.

My obesity continued through diet doctors, grapefruit diets and exercise. I lost and regained so much, so often, so unsuccessfully.

In college, I found that physical education still dogged my path. Added to this was ROTC, which was required of every student in land-grant colleges. It meant that at least once a week I had to march for a minimum of two hours in uniform.

I now lived in Florida and was attending college in north-central Florida. The temperatures were often in the 90s, and I decided that I would sign up for social dancing or square dancing or bait casting to fulfill my physical education requirements. But everyone else had the same idea, so at 300 pounds I signed up for handball. It was either that or lacrosse; everything else was closed.

The first day of handball (I had confused it with boxball and was amazed at the three-sided court) was a killer. It started gently and as the ball moved with more rapidity, I found that I was required to do so as well. Within thirty minutes I had passed out cold. I had been rolled — no one would have attempted to lift me — under a cement table on the court. It was the only shade available.

ROTC was similar. I did register a "Here, sir," before toppling. I remember the first aid kit used by coaches and ROTC commanders. It was a plastic bottle filled with water which they squirted into my eyes.

However, the fainting kept recurring and I became a habitue of the below-the-cement-table arena. But what happened in ROTC was worse. I was moved to the "sick and lame" class.

Everyone was bandaged, broken or battered at sick and lame, as frequenters knew it. Then there was "the fainter." It was demoralizing. But I could not give up my food, so I accepted this and more.

I was referred to a major medical clinic where a doctor, who I'm sure kept his instruments in the refrigerator, investigated every inch of my body and told me as I sat in the altogether on his examining table, "Your problem is that all your organs are sagging."

What do you say to such a diagnosis? "Thank you."

"We'll have to lift those organs up-up-up so that you can function," he continued.

I envisioned myself walking around holding my stomach up-up-up. "How?" I queried.

"An elastex brace," was the response. I knew he meant a girdle.

Since there were no men's girdles size 52, I chose a size 46 and decided to cut physical education. I was going to make my comeback on the ROTC field!

I poured myself into that girdle and the compliments flew when I walked to the field. I moved like a penguin, talked like a parakeet and was hyperventilating before I reached the field.

I never made rollcall. When they tried to revive me they thought I was dead. I was stiff (the girdle had very little give). I was lifted sans stretcher and awoke once again in the sick and lame class. They had leaned me against a wall, being unable to bend me.

And yet, I would not give up my food. They moved me to an inactive unit and gave me special phys ed. But I would not give up my food.

After graduation the diet club route took off 100 pounds and tapped into an incredible ego problem I didn't know existed. At 200 plus, I married and soon started to regain the weight.

Two hundred pounds later, at a size 62, I found OA. At absolute rock bottom emotionally, physically and spiritually, I walked into a room and fourteen women greeted me with smiles and joy.

They talked about "turning it over," "one day at a time" and "this too shall pass." I was sure I had walked into the wrong room, but to show them my intellectuality I retorted, "A bird in the hand is worth two in the bush," and "A penny saved . . ." They weren't interested. They just stared at me.

The first speaker I heard was a woman from Al-Anon. I knew I had made a mistake. Alcoholics have problems; I just needed a diet. She talked about resentments, fears, anger — none of which I chose to relate to.

I had been turned off by the praying at the beginning of the meeting (the Serenity Prayer by any other name is still praying). They announced "pitches" and a woman got up and proceeded to cry before the entire group.

At 400 pounds I tried to blend into the woodwork. I was mortified. Emotion, in front of everyone? Thank God they announced a coffee break. I had concluded to grab a sweet roll and go home.

No sweet rolls, no milk, nothing but black coffee greeted me. I tried to leave as unobtrusively as a 400-pounder can.

A tiny woman came over to me with a kindly smile. "Who is your sponsor?" she asked.

I had listened to nothing — no readings, no pitches, nothing. "Proctor and Gamble," I responded.

She hurriedly wrote her name on a sheet of paper and told me to call her at six the following morning.

When I arrived home and announced that I had to call a woman at six o'clock in the morning, my wife asked, "For how long?"

I hadn't listened to anything at the meeting, so I

said, "I think forever."

The next morning was different. I awoke at six, dialed the phone and was greeted by a cheery "Good morning." I thought she had stayed all night at the meeting.

My first test came within two weeks. I was on jury duty miles from any OA meeting or person. I walked into a restaurant for lunch and I knew this was it. I didn't believe in God and had rebuffed my sponsor's spiritual advances at every turn.

When lunch came I stared at the enormous portion. I had nowhere to turn. I looked up and said, "I don't believe you're there. I know for a fact if you were you wouldn't be here with me in this restaurant. But my sponsor said to 'act as if,' so that's what I'll do. I will cut this portion in half. One half is yours and the other half is mine."

It was ludicrous. I realized I was being watched. (I later came to believe that it was He who was watching.)

I never finished my half portion. The same test the next day had the same result. He had removed the obsession because I had asked.

My life changed. My world changed and my perspective changed. Suddenly, I was a vibrant, viable human being with hopes, strengths and experiences.

During my first year, I believed if you had one extra stringbean you had taken back your will and God would walk away from you. By the end of my second year of abstinence I knew God was there all the time no matter what your will was for you.

The third year the pink cloud ended and day-to-day living within God's plan took over. I threw myself more and more into OA service. This was the work God had showed me needed to be done. "Freely have you been given . . ." I had to keep giving.

The more I gave the more I received. I knew now that food had never filled the void. The twelve steps of recovery and the Big Book were the answer. The bedrock on which both rest is spirituality.

God could and would if I let Him.

It is five years, and I am still letting Him — one day at a time.

13

Thin Is Not Healthy

HE MEDICAL DIAGNOSIS was anorexia nervosa —
whatever that meant. All I knew was that the
doctor told me I had to snap out of my depression and
gain weight immediately or I'd have to be hospitalized.

I didn't feel anything was wrong with me. Yes, I was
tired and not interested in much, and I had lost a lot of
weight. But I had been trying to lose weight. What I refused to see was that I was five feet, seven inches and
weighed less than 90 pounds! Thin was beautiful; it
was the way to be accepted and admired.

How I got that way I can't really say. I had grown up
the oldest of two children in a typical middle class family. My father worked long hours as a produce shipper
and I rarely saw him. When I did, he was usually drinking. My mother stayed home, rather unhappily, until

my brother and I were in school. Then she returned to teaching.

With both my parents working, I began feeling fairly responsible, at least in some areas. I made an effort to be a good student and model daughter. I avoided getting into any of the usual kid or teenage trouble, and I remained fairly naive about the world in general.

In my senior year in high school, I came to the conclusion that I was getting too fat. I weighed about 135 pounds at the time, and at my height, I looked a little chunky. I didn't like my appearance, but I couldn't change my facial features or my height or build. If I lost weight, perhaps I would be popular; perhaps people would like me; perhaps someone might even love me.

I started dieting and, being a perfectionist, I didn't know how or when to stop. I became a walking computer who knew the calorie count of everything eatable — how much to allow myself and exactly what I'd eaten every single day.

I watched the scale go down gradually. The more I lost, the happier I was and the less I ate. I can still remember the last day of my final exams. As I walked home that day, all I could think of was, "The last three days I have eaten only diet jello and a total of less than five hundred calories."

My parents were beginning to get worried. I had lost about 25 pounds and still seemed as active as ever, but there was no indication that I planned to stop. I wasn't eating with them anymore. I prepared separate meals and refused to go out to eat. As often as possible, I also avoided going out with friends.

By the end of the summer, I weighed about 100 pounds. I was more active than ever, and dieting even more intensely. My mother finally convinced me to see a doctor because my menstrual cycle had stopped completely. The doctor could find no physical reason for either the weight loss or the menstrual problem.

The next stop was a psychiatrist. He talked about Freud, hating my mother and philosophical theories for about three months at $50 per half hour. I was getting a little upset over the whole thing, when he finally gave me his medical diagnosis and ultimatum. Anorexia nervosa sounded pretty formidable, but at least he didn't say I had to gain weight; he just told me to get over my depression.

Shock therapy was the latest "cure" for depression, and I was scheduled for six to nine treatments. After the first one, I was receptive to almost anything — including food. I was fed goodies every few hours and I didn't care. Two more sessions and 8 pounds later, I was sent home with a good prognosis. It lasted all of two months. I dropped back down to my 90 pounds and continued my lifestyle.

By this time I knew I was causing a lot of worry to a number of people. My skeletonlike figure and yellow coloring were hard for anyone to look at. So I decided to go away to finish my schooling. I applied and was accepted at a university about 150 miles from home. I threw myself into my studies so I wouldn't have to face social situations that required me to eat. I had always been a good student, but now studying became an obsession and an avoidance for facing anything else.

Somehow I maintained my 90-pound weight and top grades until I graduated two years later. There was a demand at the time for my area of study, and I obtained a good position. I threw myself into my work just as I had my studies, and tried to avoid looking at myself.

Being thin hadn't enabled me to fulfill my need for popularity, acceptance or love. I now thought that perhaps marriage would. There was a man who, surprisingly enough, wanted to marry me and who actually thought I was attractive.

During the first year and a half of our marriage, I was left to my own resources. He was in the service and stationed in Hawaii with orders for Vietnam. I stayed in California working and going to school. I felt some concern because I didn't want my husband to discover what I was really like. So I began eating a bit, and to my horror I found I liked it. I liked it so much I had trouble stopping.

It wasn't bad at first. It was a meal or two here and there, but I began putting on weight. Since I had always been so thin, I received a lot of encouragement. I began to feel as though things were going to be all right after all.

When my husband finally got out of the service, we settled down to a "normal" life. But I wasn't satisfied. Something was missing. I loved my work, liked my house (as long as I didn't have to clean it), felt OK about my marriage, but something was wrong.

For one thing, I had a very poor self concept. I hated the looks of my body. It didn't matter whether it was thin or fat, I still hated it. I could not accept myself as a woman or in any type of "womanly" role. I didn't like sex, refused to use cosmetics or dress well unless absolutely necessary, and I avoided housework. To top it off, I felt bored and restless.

I turned to the things that had usually calmed me before: food, work and school. I buried myself in work and classes and occasionally came up for air long enough to have a food binge. It was on those days that I enjoyed my husband's company because he would generally join in my eating activities, at least for part of the day. What he didn't see was what I ate while he was gone, and what he couldn't understand was my depression afterward. Once introduced to binge eating, I loved it. I began starving myself for two to three weeks to build up a big enough weight loss to "afford" the binge.

It worked for awhile, but it became progressively harder to control. The weight was going up slowly and my self-esteem was rapidly plunging. I decided to go back to school in Arizona to finish my doctorate degree and to escape — from me. Only one part was accomplished. I got the degree.

Meanwhile, I divorced my husband. My excuse was that we were going in opposite directions. I wanted a career and he wanted a family. That was true as far as it went, but it wasn't far enough. I felt unworthy and worthless as a wife or a woman and I couldn't face myself, much less a husband.

Back in California, on my own, I tried to straighten out my life. I spent another year and a half binging and starving. But my previous control was slipping. I hardly remembered my too-thin days. I began resorting to fad diets between binges, then shots, hypnosis, diuretics and anything that sounded promising. I returned to a psychiatrist, but he didn't listen to my weight problem. He wanted to straighten out my thinking. Imagine that!

I was getting desperate because the binges were lasting longer than one day. They had stretched to two or three days and they were affecting my work. I found myself making excuses to leave meetings in order to sneak food. I felt in a constant state of turmoil.

After one extremely bad three-day binge during which I ate nonstop every waking moment, I was totally devastated. I picked up the phone and called a psychiatric hotline. They asked if I was suicidal. When I said no, they said they'd call back later. I was frantic. Then I remembered something a friend had said: "If you're really in a bad way, try praying about it."

I had rejected God a long time before, but that day I

was ready to try anything. Without much hope I said, "Help me, please. It's the worst problem I've got. I can't control the food anymore. Please, help."

Somehow I made it through the day and the next with relative calm. On Friday of that week I was to go shopping with my prayer-suggesting friend. We got halfway down the block and turned around. He wanted to catch something on the news before we went. He never saw whatever it was he wanted to see, and we never made it shopping. That night on the news there was an interview with an OA member.

I felt as if I'd just had my last "shock treatment" from a most gentle Source. I knew that I was supposed to see that program, and by Monday I was at my first meeting. Tuesday I began abstinence and a whole new outlook on life.

It was almost as if I had released a valve on a pressure cooker. These people accepted me skinny or fat, good or bad, idiosyncracies and all. They also helped me get in closer contact with that Higher Power that got me to OA in the first place. Between the group with its support and love and the contact with my Higher Power, my world and my life are coming back into focus, and I'm reaching out for new opportunities.

Anorexia nervosa is often fatal. I thank God that He has seen fit to allow me an opportunity to share and grow in OA and, even more important perhaps, to be of help to my fellows who still suffer. Believe me, thin is not healthy!

14

It Ran in the Family

WHEN I WAS SEVEN, my mother nearly died and I, the oldest of three children, was "farmed out" for most of one school year. Until that time, I had been a thin, asthmatic child who didn't care about food. During my mother's illness I stayed with three different families and I gained so much weight that when I came back home my family nicknamed me "Butterball."

I was brought up in a rural part of the Midwest that never really shook off the Depression. Bible Belt Baptists, my family on both sides could be divided into two groups: grossly overweight women who were compulsive overeaters and skinny men who were alcoholics. Naturally, I identified with the women, especially my big, diabetic grandmother whose fate I always believed I would share.

I never felt close to my mother, who couldn't show love and was constantly critical, but at thirteen I made friends with a fine, loving neighbor woman who gave me my first real feeling of acceptance. Like my relatives, she was obese.

Throughout my years at home, my mother forced me to go on unpalatable or bizarre diets to keep my weight down. I was a size 14 or 16 during most of my teen years, but she made me feel so ugly and fat that in my mind there was no difference between that size and the 26½ I was ultimately to become.

In college, I was able to keep my weight at a reasonable level until my senior year, when I had my first sexual experiences. This triggered an anxiety reaction and I went up to 180 pounds in a few months. That weight seemed the end of the world to me and, for the first time, I went on a diet voluntarily. Meantime, I stopped dating and the weight came off easily.

The next year I went to graduate school in the east. I was desperately lonely because I didn't fit in with the sophistication, and I became rather promiscuous. In one school year I went from a size 14 to a 20½. That was the beginning of years of misery, because I never again got below that size and never again felt like a normal person until I got to Overeaters Anonymous at age thirty-five.

The intervening years were marked by depression, self-hatred and the steady upward toll of pounds. I was in therapy for depression for at least ten years, always thinking I ate because I was depressed, not admitting to myself that the reverse was true: I was depressed because I ate. I ate on the way to therapy and I ate after therapy, and hardly ever talked about my weight or the food with any of my therapists. I would only talk about it when I was dieting, just as the only time I ever got on the scale was when I had been dieting for at least two weeks. Denial was my big defense.

The diets I tried were the same ones everyone tries. I even had a staple in my ear once, put there by an osteopath "acupuncturist" who told me to wiggle my ear anytime I wanted to eat. Most of the time I wiggled after I ate, so it didn't do any good. I never tried diet pills. I considered myself too good and pure and drug-free for that, so I just kept on drugging myself daily with sugar and gaining more weight.

I could lose 40 pounds in six weeks anytime I chose, but since that was inevitably followed by a 50-pound gain in a few months' time, I gradually gave up dieting altogether. I had become interested in astrology and I convinced myself that my chart showed I was doomed to a lifetime of obesity.

On the surface, my life was successful. I lived in a lovely house, I was dating a beautiful, sensitive man who loved me, and I had my first book in the process of publication. I had finally arranged my career so that I could work at home most of the time, as I had always wanted to do. But I was binging and gaining weight, and when I topped 280, I wanted to kill myself.

The last straw — or perhaps the first step toward OA — was another look at my astrology chart. It was all set up for a repeat of the conditions that had coincided with a 100-pound weight gain twelve years earlier. I was within binging distance of 300 pounds.

I started a last-ditch effort at dieting. I threatened myself that if it didn't work I'd have to go to Overeaters Anonymous which a friend had told me about. Strangely enough, though I loved Alcoholics Anonymous (a close friend is a recovering alcoholic and he had taken me to a few meetings), OA sounded grim. I had been impressed with AA and had even begun to absorb some of the philosophy; still, I was sure OA couldn't do me any good.

Having flopped miserably at my "last ditch" diet, I binged my way through one last holiday season. Early in January, I dragged myself through a snowstorm to my first OA meeting.

I was not one of those people who achieve instant abstinence. My emotional reaction in those first few weeks was like unleashing a cyclone of pain. It meant facing all the feelings I used to eat to hide such as anger, loneliness, desire — and the way it feels to say yes to people when I really want and need to say no.

I stubbornly resisted taking a sponsor. The image of my controlling, dominating mother and her forced diets made my defiance very powerful on this point. I kept turning it over in meetings, as I was told, and gradually felt more at peace with it. It wasn't until two months into the program, when I was approaching my usual 40-pound turnaround point, that I began to see I had to take a sponsor if I wanted to keep what the program was giving me. Finally, my Higher Power got impatient with my shillyshallying and moved a fine woman who had been watching my struggles to ask if I wanted her to sponsor me. I accepted fearfully — she seemed so forbiddingly strict — and within a week I had my abstinence!

I lost weight at a dizzying pace: 110 pounds and twelve sizes in nine months. The food was comfortable most of the time — more comfortable, I had to admit, than my new body and my new identity. As much as I had fantasized about becoming a normal-size person, I was terrified when it actually happened.

Passing from a size 18 to a 16 was a real crisis; it seemed to symbolize crossing the barrier between being a freaky, fat person and joining the human race. People would say, "You must be so happy," and I couldn't honestly say yes. For about a month, I was incredibly uptight, fearful and uncomfortable. I discov-

ered I was afraid of men, and I also isolated myself
emotionally from everyone — in program and out.

I handled this the same way I have handled each
crisis I faced since joining OA. (Crises don't stop just
because I'm abstinent.) I work the program twice as
hard. There isn't a tool I don't use. I go to more meetings and make sure I turn over exactly what's bother-
ing me. It helps. I listen at meetings as though my life
depends on it — because it does. I especially listen to
people with similar problems and I home in like a laser
beam on people who have relapsed, because it can
happen to me if I don't learn from others' mistakes. I
make phone calls. I pray for guidance. I write out my
feelings and then burn what I've written. It's like burn-
ing old, self-defeating attitudes, and while they burn I
pray that these attitudes will change. When I apply all
aspects of the program to a crisis and trust that it is a
phase rather than a life sentence, the crisis passes.

When the food thoughts come, I take them as feelings, not commands to be acted on. In fact, a little way
into the program I learned that I forced food down
when I didn't even want it. I often ate when I was
merely thirsty. I realized that sometimes when I was
binging I didn't even like the food; it became an
enormous burden to consume it all. Now, I try to make
mealtime serene and pleasant. I say a simple grace before each meal: "God, thank you for this beautiful food,
and thank you that I don't have to eat too much of it."

I have become contented with my new body and my
new identity. Now, when people say, "You must be so
happy," I practically sing out that I really am. I'm still
startled when I see myself in a mirror or store window,
and I can still be moved to tears by a medium size that
fits. I no longer have the self-loathing that comes with
feeling like a freak. The male attention I am getting
amazes and pleases me. I have become used to all this,

but I am not complacent; just comfortable and very grateful. I have a life to look forward to instead of a living death.

In a sense, the body changes, wonderful as they are, are superficial. The most important gift of the program is a way to deal with life. People who are compulsive have learned only one response to stress: for the alcoholic the response is drink; for the overeater it is food. Whatever the stress, we ate. It didn't really help that much, but we didn't know what else to do. Now I know what to do: I work my program, and it helps in a way food never did. Not only do I feel better for the moment, but my life gets better, too. It's a wonderful feeling.

15

The Keys To Freedom

*M*Y STORY IS A simple one. As I listen in meetings I find how much alike I am to others. This comes as a surprise because for many years I felt I was different.

My first memory is of being given food to make me feel better, and I was quite happy to get it. I taught myself to cook at an early age because my mother worked fulltime and it was the only way I could get what I wanted. I badgered my parents when they wouldn't supply me, and I stole food whenever I thought I could get away with it. I had to work hard to maintain my compulsive overeating.

Because I was obese, I was teased as a child and I withdrew from people. As an only child, I found it relatively easy to become a recluse. I lived in a world of my own in which imaginary friends and television were my only companions.

In the real world I was a battered child. My parents both worked and they had turned my care over to a maid. This woman would beat me at unpredictable times. I never told my parents because I felt that I deserved to be punished. My parents were having trouble at the time and they often had long, bitter arguments. In my child's mind I believed these problems were my fault, so I took the beatings by the maid as a kind of penitence for all the trouble I thought I was causing.

My parents thought my bruises were the result of normal childhood accidents. When they discovered the truth, they fired the maid. But three years of physical abuse left quite an impression on me.

My self-concepts were seriously out of line. I remember when I was nine years old I went to see a great uncle whom I had never met. When he saw me, he picked me up and threw me into the air. I thought he was either God or Superman. I couldn't believe that anyone could do that. I thought I was so large, I was immovable. Like my great uncle, Overeaters Anonymous has lifted me up when I thought I was beyond help.

When I was thirteen, my parents decided it wasn't baby fat anymore and took me to a doctor for a diet. Having gotten into trouble at school, I was also taken to a psychiatrist. I lost 30 pounds on the doctor's diet by simply not eating. However, I soon became ill and I had to eat in order to get well. I gained all the weight back — and more. I didn't think much of the diet, but I loved the cure.

The psychiatrist was just about as successful. I sat for six years in silence in her office. I trusted no one, yet I wanted desperately for her to help me. She kept telling my parents that since I refused to talk I didn't have to go back, but I continued to return. I didn't have anyplace else to go.

When I was fifteen my father, whom I worshipped, had a nervous breakdown. He had entered the hospital a relatively young man of forty and came out three months later with gray hair, walking with a cane and looking like a man twenty years older. I grieved for him. For an entire summer I stayed in the house, going from my bedroom to the kitchen. The only time I went out was to visit the psychiatrist. My weight shot up dramatically.

The psychiatrist suggested that I would be better off somewhere else, so I went to live with my aunt and uncle. I wanted to change, but I didn't know how. My way was to go on a diet. I didn't know how much I weighed because I refused to get on a scale. After dieting for some time, I did weigh myself and found the scale registering 212. I lost another 55 pounds, but I made no other change in myself so the weight didn't stay off.

The remainder of my high school years were filled with depression and self-imposed loneliness. I learned to live one day at a time in a negative sense. I dragged myself through each day living only for the time I could eat. During this period I came very close to committing suicide.

When I went to college, I tried to get out and be with people. I went to a girls' school and found that everybody was dieting. I made friends by going on whatever diet the other girls happened to be on. Eventually, I even began dating.

I have learned since coming to OA that whatever we turn to in times of trouble is our higher power. I turned to food and when food didn't help, I turned to diets. If food wouldn't make things better, then being thin would. In college I began to diet compulsively. My weight went down, but it never stayed down for long. I wanted desperately to be like everybody else but I felt that I was so different it was impossible. I thought if I were married, I would be normal. I wanted people to do for me what I could not do for myself.

In my senior year in college, I was faced with the prospect of going out on my own. I met a man who was willing to marry me and within a year of that marriage I had gone up over 200 pounds and I had become a battered wife. I accepted this as a fate I deserved.

My husband hated my obesity, and I hated myself. I was not a pleasant person to be with. I tried dieting with and without pills. Nothing worked. Once, in pastoral counseling, I lost 75 pounds. But the counseling ended, and the diet wore out. Within six months I had regained all the weight.

I joined a commercial diet club and became a compulsive weight watcher. If the club didn't have an opinion on a topic, I didn't either. I lost the weight again over a period of two years. Finally I left because I felt there had to be more to life than weighing in every week.

My weight began to climb again. I knew I needed help but everything had failed. I had read about OA in Ann Landers' column. I believed in two things: food and Ann Landers. She had said that OA worked, so I decided to try it. There was one problem, however. I didn't know where OA was. I decided that if I ever stumbled over OA or if it ever fell on top of me, I would look into it.

A couple of months later I heard a spot announcement for OA on the radio, but I took no action. I waited a week before I called the radio station. "You don't still have the telephone number for Overeaters Anonymous, do you?" I asked. They did.

At my first meeting, I decided I didn't want to get mixed up with a bunch of religious fanatics. All I wanted was a diet and I didn't see how God could help there. However, I believed in Ann Landers, so I kept coming back.

I thought it would be enough just to attend meetings. I tried to play my old game which was to sit and say nothing. The people made no demands on me, though they seemed to care and some even telephoned me. However, I had a secret. *They* were the compulsive overeaters, not I. I knew how to lose weight. All I needed was a little group support.

For nine months I attended meetings and gained 35 pounds. I kept waiting for something to happen that would make me not want to eat anymore. It didn't. We were a small group and since I always came back, I was asked to get involved in service. That kept me coming back when I lost faith in Ann Landers. I also listened. I began to see that the people who were trying to make the steps a part of their lives were changing and good things were happening to them. I wanted that, too.

The insanity of my disease was evident to everyone but me. My life was in shambles. I had gained weight while attending meetings regularly, and I had no reason to believe that it would stop. I hated my job. I teach, and my students were noticing my weight gain. My marriage was not bliss, either. Yet I thought all I needed was a diet!

I went back to the doctor, who made it clear that he could offer me nothing new. I even returned to the diet club, but I could not sit through the lectures. In desperation, I went back into therapy. After a binge, I told the therapist about it and wanted to know what she was going to do about it. To my amazement, she said she didn't have any magic cures and that if I were truly a compulsive overeater I'd better get back to OA and do exactly what they told me.

I had no choices left. I made a decision to test the program. I challenged this Higher Power to get me through a day of abstinence. I lived through the day and nobody was more surprised than I was. That evening I went to a meeting and the speaker said, "When all else fails, follow directions." The directions were to get a sponsor, read the literature, use the telephone, act "as if," and use the steps. I got a sponsor at the end of the meeting and by the grace of God I have been abstinent from that time to this — a period of five years. I lost the 40 pounds I needed to lose the first year and I have been maintaining my normal weight since then. Before the program I never kept weight off for more than three days.

My progress has been slow. For the first few months the food plan was my higher power. However, I began to turn small things over. When I had done everything I could and felt nothing worse could happen, I would turn the problem over without regard to who or what would take it. To my amazement, every time I did this something good followed. My belief that a Higher Power — God — could help me came slowly, but it came.

Step three came when, in an effort to help someone else, I memorized the third-step prayer on page 63 in the Big Book. I didn't understand it or even believe it at first, but I repeated it daily. Finally, after being abstinent for almost a year, I could feel the surrender and it was beautiful. The longer I am in the program the more the impact of this prayer grows and deepens within me. For the first time in my life I am free to deal with life without having to resort to the indignity of using food to get me through.

I continued in therapy, and for the first time it was working. The therapy helped me to be open to OA, and OA helped me to be open to therapy. After a year and a half of abstinence, I took my fourth and fifth steps with my therapist. Much to my surprise (and disappointment) she didn't turn green or faint. From this, I was able to go to people in OA and share.

I became willing to have my defects of character removed. These defects were comfortable and I hung onto them dearly. I never knew it was OK to be happy. Someone had to tell me. The old comfortable, familiar pain has gradually given way to peace. I am not perfect, but I have been granted the gifts of change and growth. I know now that with the help of my Higher Power I am no longer locked into a prison of unhappy ways. The program has given me the keys to freedom.

I have learned two important things. One is that life may bring pleasure or it may bring pain, but the program has given me the tools to deal with whatever comes. I have also learned that life is to be enjoyed. I spend time in meetings and doing twelfth-step work which brings me both peace and joy. I am also able to go out into the world and be at peace there, too.

16

Journey through Deception

$\mathcal{B}$EFORE I CAME THROUGH the OA door five years ago, I had done little about my weight problem. I blamed my sluggish metabolism. I complained that other people could eat more than I did without gaining a pound.

Life was so unfair!

Years ago I discovered that when I kept busy the weight melted off without any conscious effort on my part. So I started a cycle that alternated between distraction and depression for the next twenty years. While busy, I maintained a low weight of 120 pounds. When the distraction lost its charm, as it inevitably did, I became depressed and immobilized. My weight would skyrocket, rising higher with each slump.

At five feet, three inches, I weighed 178 pounds. I know this only because I visited a diet club where they

95

weighed me. Normally I shunned scales, mirrors and cameras so that I could keep my self-deceptions intact. I went through my fat periods in a state of isolation and suspension, waiting till I could become "real" again with another spate of activity.

Five years ago I was in another slump. This time I could not afford to wait for something to spur me out of it. I was facing possible bankruptcy and had two lawsuits pending. It might be years before these were settled. I had to come to terms with my weight problem now. I had no experience with other diet systems, but the choice was easy: I was broke and OA was free.

From the time of my first meeting I abstained and called my food in daily to the sponsor I chose that night. The food plan I adopted was a new game to me and by playing it I lost 52 pounds in four and a half months. My "tools" were diet pop, artificial sweeteners and nail biting. I went to many meetings, but treated them as living soap operas. I tuned out what I thought of as the "religious" part of the program. I stayed aloof because I did not want to identify with losers, i.e. compulsive overeaters. I was there to lose weight, not to change my personality or get religion. I thought my personality was just fine, and I already believed in a loving God.

When my weight got down to 120 pounds, I left OA with my slim body and my fat head.

I continued to abstain by myself and lost four more pounds. I was filled with complacence: I had the magic formula and I could do it alone! For the next two and a half years I weighed myself daily, kept a log of everything I ate and "passed" as a thin person. Certainly, I never gave any credit to OA.

I did learn three things from that first experience with OA: to follow a food plan; to be aware of what I ate; and never to overeat because of guilt about overeating. I applied the discipline I had learned from abstinence to other areas of my life and was quite sucessful. My new job was the best I had ever had. I learned sports and tried my hand at new hobbies such as dressmaking. Every relationship in my life bloomed. I never looked or felt better.

But something was missing. Toward the end of this period my weight began to climb until it reached 142 pounds. The new pants I had just made soon would not fit.

Back I came to OA, more desperate, less cocky, more willing. While I had been away I had given up my "tools." I decided not to take them back. This time I would be forced to work the program instead of transferring my compulsions. This time, if I blew it, I knew it would be with food.

I began by attacking my self-serving deceptions.

I had no metabolism problem. My glands worked just as well at one weight as another.

I couldn't blame heredity. True, my mother and sisters were compulsive overeaters, but my father always ate moderately and kept his normal weight.

I couldn't blame my attitudes toward food on my conditioning. My mother had served large portions and insisted that I finish them. But millions of youngsters are given too much to eat and are urged to finish it because "wasting food is a sin," yet they do not wind up gorging themselves. It was true that it pleased my mother to see me enjoy her cooking. But I rebelled against her authority in other ways constantly and felt no compunction about not pleasing her.

It had not been my parents who told me to devour my lunch on the way to school, to steal candy from neighbors, to take nickels from my mother's purse for candy bars. They told me candy was junk and stealing was wrong.

I could not blame lack of parental love either. I assumed guilt by association when my mother told me that my birth coincided with her goiter operation, which left an ugly scar. I believed myself rejected when my father said that before my birth he was fearful about the Depression and really didn't want another child. I took up martyrdom because my parents gave me approval only when I was polite and obedient, and they seemed unable to accept my feelings.

But I came to realize that most people are raised with conditional love; that nearly everyone is sometimes made to feel inferior by his parents; that many men and women lack self-worth. But they do not become overeaters. While I cleared my head of these old tapes, I had to abstain.

I could not blame my compulsion on the burdens I had grown up with. I was born with some physical abnormalities. My mother and sister were psychotic. My brother was mentally retarded. My father deserted his family when I was twelve, and we were destitute. We lived in a slum where violence was commonplace. Food was my bit of sweetness in such misery.

But I have learned to live with each of these facts and I have grown stronger because of them. Others have just as much to contend with and they do not choose to eat over it. Living in the past, bemoaning my fate is just a way to justify my eating.

I have learned to see myself as one of God's children, neither the best nor the worst. I know I have talent, intelligence and ability, and I have had many fine accomplishments. But my self-worth is not validated by any of these. I can love and accept my weaknesses as well as my strengths because they are part of me. I make many mistakes as I reach toward growth, but I no longer expect perfection from myself or anyone else.

Despite this acceptance, I am still tempted at times

to kill myself by overeating. My loving self has to work a very tough program to prevent my destroying self from taking over.

I have learned to value more of the simple things, such as the sheer joy of being alive. My happiness depends on my attitude, not on circumstances. Whether I am a compulsive overeater or not, life presents daily problems; how happy I want to be while dealing with them is up to me.

I know now that my immature personality was the root of my problem and that growing up was the solution. I learned to accept my feelings and to take responsibility for channeling them constructively. I went through the steps. I became more patient, compassionate and honest. The changes in me brought loving responses from those around me. My weight dropped to 105 pounds.

But I had more to learn. It was painful to realize that my feelings were not the cause of my eating. I had gone through temper tantrums, guilt, loneliness, resentment, fear — many negative emotions — all my life. I overate not because of the feelings, but because I was food-obsessed and I gave myself license to overeat by producing the negative emotions. In other words, I made myself upset so that I had an excuse to overeat.

I may never be emotionally mature. This is an endless journey. But while I travel on it, I cannot use my lack of maturity to justify my eating. Emotional and physical binges are no longer substitutes for action.

I see now that the alternative to abstinence, for me, is suicide. I am no longer able to tell myself lies to excuse binges. In order to abstain, I keep these things in mind: 1. I believe, for today, that I must compensate for my lack of food brakes by maintaining those disciplines that enable me to be moderate. 2. For me, one bite of certain carbohydrates is suicide, fast or slow, because I lack psychosomatic immunity to them. 3. I cannot indulge in negativity, because it blocks out my program awareness. Self-pity is a luxury I cannot afford because it causes amnesia, and I revert to old habits. 4. My primary responsibility is to abstain. All roles — wife, mother, friend, employee — come second. If abstinence is not first, I will lose it. Everything that interferes with it must go. 5. I never have it made. My compulsion never goes away; it waits for me to become careless or cocky. 6. The OA program at its toughest is better than binging. Life at its dreariest or scariest is better than death by overeating.

I am continuing to discard more lies. I have the love of OA friends and my family in making this painful, joyous journey. I am grateful because I know that getting rid of deceptions makes me freer to see the ones that still blind me, still bind me.

17

Fat Is Not My Destiny

*F*OOD WAS A FAMILY affair. My brothers and I were born in the years following World War II and we were caught up in the race for affluence and security, one symbol of which was unlimited food. Any occasion called for a feast: birthdays, holidays, vacations, Sunday excursions, births, deaths, weddings, reunions. Once the basic overeating pattern was established, I elaborated on it. No matter where I went to school there was always a store or pastry shop or candy counter I could patronize, and I resorted to stealing nickels and dimes and quarters from my father's change box to supplement my inadequate allowance.

At home I ate anything I could get my hands on, straight from the box, can or jar, cooked or uncooked, baked or unbaked; it made no difference. I had no discriminating tastes. Canned spaghetti tasted as delicious to me as any treasured Italian family recipe. I couldn't even appreciate my German grandmother's baking as any better than Sara Lee's. I lost babysitting jobs because I ate everything except the baby.

My compulsive overeating may have had something to do with my older brother's chronic illness. He spent his entire childhood in and out of hospitals and my parents were preoccupied with his health. Just as his disease was brought under control and I was struggling through adolescence, my younger brother developed schizophrenia, and my parents' concern shifted to him. Somehow, in the midst of all this, food became my reward and punishment, love and companionship.

By the time I was in high school, I weighed 150 pounds, a weight below which I have never fallen in my adult life. I carried it well — in the same place a barrel does — and the straight skirts, tucked-in blouses and belted shirtwaists then in fashion made it impossible to disguise.

I never dated, and I quickly resigned myself to cutting remarks and snickers when my stomach growled in class. I eventually kept mostly to myself to avoid getting hurt, and I convinced myself that this was the way I wanted it.

After graduating from college, I became a high school librarian in a small school. I moved in with two college friends who were also teaching there and was ready to believe I had it made for the rest of my life. During the second year, reality set in and teaching became a serious business. Soon it deteriorated into a battle. My first major disappointment was the realization that I was not going to make it in the profession. I didn't see the pattern building until it was too late, but that failure made me resentful and angry. I was angry at the kids because in spite of my best efforts to direct and control their lives, they failed me and that reflected on me. I was angry at the principal, whom I considered incompetent; I was angry at the other teachers who seemed successful; I was angry at my parents because I believed they had pressured me into teaching; and I was angry at myself for letting things get out of control, including my weight which had gone up 38 pounds in four years.

I fought it every way I could, from letters to Dear Abby to psychiatric counseling, from memberships in health spas and diet clubs to books on losing weight. Nothing worked. Everything emphasized food. I was still looking forward to eleven o'clock for the celery sticks, counting the minutes until I could eat the apple I had saved from lunch, planning menus and substitutions that read like computer printouts. As an example of my obsessiveness, I had by that time collected forty-three cookbooks and nine shoeboxes of clipped recipes. (You won't find this food emphasis in OA. The emphasis is on you and me and us as people, not on food.)

The amazing thing about this most important time in my life is that through it all I never even knew I was angry. I mean, after all, everybody else was failing me; it was their fault, not mine. Lord knows I was trying. Outwardly, I was controlled, calm, in command. Inwardly, the growing anger was eating me up and I was trying to stop it with food.

It was inevitable that a crisis would occur with such pressures building, and in my fifth and final year of teaching it did. I almost killed a student in one blinding moment of anger that broke through. In February of that year, I was on hall duty and enduring the usual hassles that go with the job. That particular day Tommy Troublemaker chose to make himself unbearable. I had just shooed him down the stairs for the third time, then stepped into a teacher's room. She was the play director and she showed me some of the props her people had been collecting, one of which was a heavy iron crowbar. I was standing by her desk talking, my hand on that crowbar, when Tommy sauntered through the door with some smart remark. In a flash of anger, my hand closed around the crowbar and raised it. Had the teacher not grabbed my wrist, I probably would have taken Tommy's head off, although I can't be sure of that.

I laid the crowbar back on the desk and went to the superintendent's office, where I wrote out my resignation on the back of a lunch menu and turned it in. For the three months remaining in the school year, that woman and two other good friends ran interference for me, and there were no further incidents. But I lived in fear of what might happen and in agony over what I had found out about myself.

When school was over, I moved out of the state with the sole intention of vegetating for a year and bringing myself and my weight under control. Actually, I wasn't moving to a place so much as I was moving away from people and things. Among them was a man who wanted to marry me; I thought there must be something wrong with him if he could love me.

The most joyous discovery I made upon my arrival in my new community was supermarkets that were open twenty-four hours a day. I spent my first three weeks eating and watching television, crying, depressed. I never got dressed except to go out and buy food. For the first time in my life I knew what real loneliness was.

I began going to OA meetings soon after I got settled, but my first weeks with the program were exasperating. I was disagreeable, hostile and resentful that I had to be there at all. But mostly I was frightened that if I tried to follow the program and failed there was nothing left. Also, I am agnostic and my first impression was that I had happened upon a group of evangelists who would attempt to convince me that nothing could happen until I accepted their God.

They quickly disproved that. Once I stopped looking for flaws and began listening in earnest, I was able to find a higher power that works for me. My higher power is the group, the people, my friends.

Abstinence and weight loss came only after I accepted the fact that this program is something I cannot manage alone; I need all the help I can get, and there's no shame in that.

Many other physical symptoms of overeating have disappeared. Gone are dry skin, joint pains, sinusitis, headaches. I'm off thyroid after twenty-two years. I can cross my legs under a table without causing a commotion. My knee socks come up to my knees now. These are measurements that make me feel good about myself.

Emotionally I am freer, and spiritually I am at peace with myself and with my higher power. The quality of my life is improving every day.

My salvation, if you will, came with the realization that being fat is not in my mind or my destiny, but is rather a symptom of a disease, compulsive overeating. Thanks to an incident that occurred during my first year in the program, I know that compulsive overeating is controllable, but not curable.

On that particular occasion, shortly before Christmas, I led an OA meeting during which I told the group that I was to be married — to the same man I had moved away from. I was feeling worthy for the first time in my life — open and loving. I flew to my parents' home the next day for a long weekend and felt very proud of the way I resisted temptation and handled my food while there, because Christmas at home is a feast from beginning to end. I also dealt with my family's rather hostile reaction to my marriage plans in what I considered a calm, adult manner. I even smiled benignly during all the hassles of holiday travel and returned home ready to begin a new year.

The next day I went to work and someone opened a box of chocolates. Within two hours I had eaten the entire thing, and it was supposed to have been shared among five people. I didn't feel the least bit guilty about it. After work, I drove to a mall and bought my favorite binge foods. As an example of the extremes to which compulsive overeaters are driven, I was too ashamed to eat these things in public and couldn't wait to get home, so in nine-degree weather in a car with no heat, I sat in the parking lot and ate the stuff with my gloves on and darn near froze to death.

Then I realized that within a short span of time, I was back to square one and doing the disgusting, revolting things I hated, and what was there to eat about anyway? I was happier than I had ever been in my life. I was to be married to someone I loved very much. My work was going well. I got A's in my semester course work. I had many friends. My future was bright. Why did I feel the need to punish myself this way?

I had no answer. I still don't, but that's not what matters. What matters is that I started the car and got to an OA meeting where I shared what I had just done.

OA people don't judge or react with horror when they hear something like that. They listen, they talk, they suggest readings, they call me later to see how I'm doing, they stop in the middle of their day when I call to talk. With this help and encouragement, I was able to break the vicious rationalization that because I did it once, another time won't hurt, or I'll wait until January 1st and start all over again. I started again right then, and although the compulsive feeling didn't leave me for days, I didn't eat about it. And soon I was OK.

But I got a good dose of humility which I badly needed, and the complacency I was beginning to feel was gone permanently. I know now that this job is never done. But I take it a day at a time, twelve hours at a time, sometimes fifteen minutes at a time, and that's the way I win.

18

A Hunger for Life

*O*N MY THIRTIETH birthday, I gave myself ten years to live. I was devouring phenomenal quantities of food, then making myself throw up. I couldn't stop myself — despite the ripped-up stomach, scratched throat, bleeding knuckles and grotesque lack of nourishment which I expected to kill me by the time I was forty.

Three weeks later, I found Overeaters Anonymous — and abstinence. Now I give myself ten decades to live!

I don't know exactly when my compulsive overeating began, but it was definitely a progressive disease. As a child, I was a hearty eater. In high school I was unhappy enough about my weight to drink coffee without sugar, and I ate uncontrollably while babysitting (then tried to "cover up" because I felt humiliated that so much food was missing). By college the "yo-yo syndrome" was well on its way. I went abroad during my junior year and for the first time in my life I gained weight to the point of growing out of my clothes. I was amazed — and puzzled — that I ate so much.

My compulsive overeating progressed at an alarming rate. During my senior year in college I began to question all the values of my strict religious upbringing. I became horribly depressed and suicidal, dropped out of school and spent several months in mental hospitals.

The chaos that erupted then continued for almost ten years, beginning to subside only when I became abstinent in OA nearly a decade later.

During those years I wildly and excessively did everything I had been prohibited — drinking, smoking, sex — with no new values to guide me, to tell me when to stop for my own good. I tried to commit suicide when I was twenty-one, then managed to pull myself together enough to finish college and to hold a job for two years.

Meanwhile, I had discovered that food and health are connected, so I ate healthfully for two or three months at a time, then began overeating on the most healthful of foods, slipped into the junk and was soon binging on the worst. This cycle went on for years: I would find a diet that worked until I lost the weight, then I began to overeat again — always amazed and perplexed that I did so. Each time, my weight soared higher than before.

A popular diet club gave me a ray of hope. I became slender, and began to feel much better about myself.

It was time, I decided at age twenty-seven, to confront the God question, which I had shelved all these years. I went to seminary to grapple with my religious tradition — to either chuck it or find a new understanding of it.

I became an atheist, largely because of my studies, but more because of my seeming non-experience of God. I felt that, despite my years of crying out for help, God had done absolutely nothing about my eating problem.

I had come to seminary slim and elated, but soon found myself very depressed. The last illusions had burst. Being in seminary was not enough; being thin was not enough; lovers and money and success were not enough. Nothing was enough. Everything I had achieved simply mocked me, reminding me that the problem was within.

Four months after starting seminary I "blew" the diet club, devouring quantities of junk that astounded even me. My astonished friends and professors watched me blow up enormously in a matter of days. Every other day I went out for a new pair of jeans, each the next size larger.

That was why I became an atheist. Where was God? What did God have to do with my eating compulsion? Why didn't God give me the strength to stop? For years I had been imploring God to help me, but nothing had happened — except that my compulsion kept getting worse and I kept feeling more hopeless.

I began therapy, and I am not sure I would have stayed alive long enough to find OA without it. My therapists helped me to feel the real hunger behind my compulsive overeating — the deep sadness and terror and rage and longing — and to accept the needy, insatiable baby within me. I came to accept myself, binging and all, and to know, as I often screamed out in therapy sessions, that *"I'm not bad!"* I felt a glimmer of hope that I would eventually stop escaping into food to block my feelings.

But I was afraid that I might kill myself in the process. My overeating had gotten so severe, in fact, that one night I sat in a pastry shop after a binge and decided that the only solution was to stop eating completely — to commit suicide by slow starvation. This would achieve my goal of killing myself, but it would also give therapy time to work *if* it were going to work.

Then I got the brilliant idea of numbing myself with alcohol, which I could buy with the money I'd save by not eating. I bought some liquor, returned to my lonely dorm room and drank one bottle, poured down some more, then guzzled still more. I felt so intensely the split between what I wanted to do and what I actually did that I took a knife and scratched a delicate line down the middle of my forehead and nose to symbolize that rift. Then I scratched deeper lines outward from my navel, like spokes on a wheel. (Every time I binged, I had fantasized plunging a knife into my belly, the source of my problem.) In my stupor, I scrawled a note explaining that, if I died, it was not intentionally. Even the next day I felt poisoned, and feared that I might not come out of it alive.

Shortly after, I read an article about anorexia nervosa, and learned about self-induced vomiting. Throwing up whenever I ate soon became a second agonizing compulsion.

I wanted to get my seminary degree and hightail it out of there and then never deal with God again. Much to my disliking, I still had to meet one requirement in New Testament.

After a huge binge followed by the vomiting ordeal, I bumped into a seminary professor in Central Park one summer evening. (Looking back now, I attribute that encounter to "Higher Power.") Walter told me about a course he would be teaching, utilizing art forms such as clay, body movement and painting. Since I had to take something, this seemed the most tolerable way out. I signed up, intending to make this my lowest priority, to just slip by. But I found myself getting emotionally involved in our class explorations, often angrily, sometimes longingly — never neutrally.

An abstinent day seemed like the best present I could possibly give myself for my thirtieth birthday, which ended up being a nightmare instead. (I had learned the term "abstinence" at the one OA meeting I had attended — and loathed — a few months before.) I went out and drank excessively, smoked for the first time in months, wolfed down a monstrous meal, then stocked up on plenty of junk. Drunk and stuffed but unable to wait till I got to my room, I pushed down more food on the subway. Back in my lonely room, I lit my birthday candles, then crammed in the rest of the garbage. After forcing myself to vomit, I rolled into bed, sick and despairing — thirty years old and utterly miserable.

The next day I went with Walter's class on a weekend retreat, where I expected not to be able to binge. No sooner had I arrived, however, than I was gobbling down sweets and sneaking off to make myself throw up. The next night was a repeat performance, and I crawled into my sleeping bag feeling more hopeless than ever.

We were working on some New Testament healing stories that weekend, and I had cried out my rage that they stirred up my longings to be healed, then left me hanging.

I woke up in anguish on the last day, thinking about the horror of my whole life. I began to cry. Not wanting to awaken my roommates, I went into the kitchen, where I flailed my arms furiously at God, yelling vehemently, "I hate you! I hate you! *I hate you!*" I felt as if I would break.

I was sobbing violently when Walter came in. I told him about the gobs of food and the vomiting, and asked whether he could pray "even for me." He placed his hands firmly on my head and prayed, calmly but insistently, for God to heal me and to fill me.

For about a week I ate "normally." I was elated that the "miracle" had happened. But soon I was hanging on by the fingernails, feeling as if I *had* to overeat. "This isn't healing!" I screamed disappointedly to myself and angrily to God.

I did the worst binging of my entire life during the next two weeks, and felt more despairing than ever. I had come to accept myself, binging and all, but cried out to my therapist one night, "I don't care how much I accept myself — I don't want it anymore!"

"Try OA again," she suggested.

"But I hated it!" I protested.

"Give it another try."

"OK," I sighed. What else could I do?

After therapy, I holed up in my dorm room and ate for a couple of hours, then — for the last time — I climbed up on a chair and vomited into the corner sink. (The bathroom was down the hall.) When I had finished, just after midnight, I went downstairs to a public telephone and called Overeaters Anonymous to find out where there was a meeting the next day.

That was the beginning of my progressive recovery — and of my gradual return to trust in God, in God's goodness and in prayer.

The next morning I went on a fad diet, then got to an OA meeting at noon. This time I identified with what people were sharing. I was amazed when I heard the first three steps. I had already taken them, unwittingly, with Walter! I was thrilled when the meeting ended with the Lord's prayer. (I had just learned in Walter's class that "Our Father," in its ancient form, is an infant's cry for nourishment.) I felt hopeful that I was finally in the right place, that I had come home.

I was still wary, however — afraid that this might be

just another tantalizing false hope that would leave
me more disillusioned than ever.

Still dubious about the effectiveness of prayer, I im-
plored God to give me a vegetarian sponsor. At my next
OA meeting, two days later, I expressed my need.

"You must give up your will!" a woman admonished
me, thrusting a non-vegetarian food plan under my
nose.

"God!" I screamed silently. "What am I to do?"

"I know!" whooped another woman. "Pearly."

Pearly, a vegetarian as committed to abstinence as
anyone can be, agreed to be my sponsor. I will always
be grateful to her for my life. She supported and
guided me through many difficulties and dilemmas,
always reminding me that it is worth it. Together we
grew in our firm commitment to abstinence as the
most important thing in our lives without exception.

I continue to cry out for further healing, to demand
that God fill me with other things so that I can enjoy
my food as food and nothing more. My prayers are
being answered, perhaps not in my time or in my way,
but in God's time and in God's way — which, I increasingly trust, is best.

Abstinence from compulsive overeating is the foundation upon which the rest of my life is gradually being
built. Abstinence gives me the emptiness I need so
there is room to be filled with other things. Little by
little, I am being filled with that for which I really
hunger: people, love, meaningful work, pleasurable
activities — *life.*

19

Beautiful Woman Inside and Out

*H*OW DOES ONE TELL in a few pages the story of fifteen and a half years in Overeaters Anonymous? How can I describe in a limited number of words what seven years of abstinence means coming after eight years of alternating between defiance, despair and submission to the program? How do I tell you of the gratitude in my heart for the miracles of abundance, joy, health, strength and power in my life today? Mine was a life lived in insecurity, self-doubt, chronic illness, addiction and obesity.

When people look at me today, they see a tall, attractive, slender woman. There seems to be a quality about me that many call "beautiful." It is not my outward appearance, but rather something from within that comes from living the twelve steps to the best of my ability. I could not have imagined such a gift. When I daydreamed or "prayed," it was to be thin magically and to have Prince Charming find me. I prayed for the money to pay my bills, take a trip, buy a new car and so on. Who would have thought to pray for a fullness from within that can make a spastic colon behave normally, control the chronic leg cramps and backaches and palpitations, and take away the desire for refined sugar and flour? That would be asking for miracles.

All I wanted was a nice house, a good school for my children, two cars in the garage and that I should look good on Saturday night. By praying for specific things, I was limiting the good in my life and expanding and giving power to negativity. It took many years to understand this; the gift of "life while living" came hard for me.

For years I tried frantically to prove that after I got thin I could eat anything I wanted anytime I wanted it. Always, I regained the lost weight, plus a few pounds, never being able to wear the same clothes from one season to another, always on a diet, whether eating or starving. I have known the pain and humiliation of not being able to participate in sports and of being laughed at by the other kids as well as by teachers, store clerks, strangers and even friends.

Though my recovery is not unique in Overeaters Anonymous, it may help the reader's understanding to know the specific ills from which I have recovered. To the best of my recollection, they are: food obsession, the weight yo-yo syndrome, the scale running my life, my size being my self-worth, living on fifteen pills a day (amphetamines, diuretics, laxatives), smoking three packs of cigarettes a day, drinking ten to fifteen cans of diet soda a day, drinking fifteen mugs of coffee a day, chewing three packs of sugarless gum a day, chronic leg cramps, chronic lower backaches, chronic need for excessive sleep, spastic colon.

These symptoms were a way of life for me. I believed and trusted them. They kept me guilty and failing and never achieving the good within me. While I can say that I have experienced moments of great sensual pleasure, the deep fear within me always brought me crashing to new lows. It was a price I expected to pay for grabbing and snatching at material things.

My race for possessions and sensual gratification gave me a good deal of fun and enjoyment, which is recorded with love in my memory. But the price I had to pay in self-hate, rage at my children and poor health (I never really felt well unless I was using a substance or making love) was too high.

And one day it stopped. I don't know when or how it stopped. It happened in stages, inch by inch, pound by pound. One day, after two and a half years of rigid abstinence and fear of food, I woke up and understood that I no longer had to fear sugar and flour. I know neither the time nor the process by which these dependencies were removed. I know only that when I stopped trying to control the timetable for the removal of my addictions, they were removed.

Today I celebrate seven years of abstinence, accumulated, by the grace of God, one day at a time. What does that mean to me? I have come to understand that we in OA cannot have the perfect, absolute abstinence that is common to AAs. Abstinence must be a different thing for each of us. Mine is always changing and growing, just as I change and grow to meet the world and God.

What worked for me in the beginning of my OA years is no longer valid. I had to learn that strict adherence to any food plan was madness for me if I hoped to thrive in the mainstream of life.

Today I am so filled with love and gratitude for my understanding of abstinence that I find it difficult to describe. I believe abstinence can be anything we want it to be, so long as we are honest with ourselves.

I have come to know my body inside and out, better than any doctor could know it. I have not been ill in seven years except for one brief bout with flu and a minor cold. Of course, I still go for medical checkups and I do not discount the value of medical science.

Today I am maintaining a 60-pound weight loss in the program. The twelve steps are a way of life for me, reaching into every aspect of my affairs. One year ago, my husband came to the program after fighting it for nine years. He has just completed his first year of abstinence and a 60-pound weight loss. My daughter is now in OA and actively participating in our teen program. It is a miracle in our lives and we are grateful for the abundance that has been given us.

Today I know that I have an addictive personality and that from time to time my illness will flare up. That doesn't mean I am a failure. It means I can be restored to sanity any time I choose the power. While food is no longer a problem and many outer manifestations have been removed, the illness still creeps up in emotional storms and maladjustments. That is the nature of life, and I grow from working through each experience.

There are many things that are "right" with me today, starting with the Higher Power that is at work in my life. It is a Power that is within me, the highest self I can be, whom I choose to call God. God in my life is expressed through many channels, and I have a receiver that is turned on, thanks to the program. Some of the channels through which I receive God are music, poetry, literature, art, dance, people, nature, forces for good in the universe and love. Love is surely an expression of a Higher Power in my life. Today I can give and receive love—and know that, by the grace of God, I am a beautiful woman inside and out.

20

The Roulette Player

I WAS RAISED IN AN alcoholic home amidst the usual tension, chaos, fear and violence that drinking provokes. When I was twelve I discovered the perfect sedative: food. Eating enormous amounts of sugary "treats" presented no problem until I started to gain weight.

I was terrified of being fat because I knew it would make me even more unacceptable than I was. With my protruding front teeth, big ears, acne and shyness, who needed another handicap? The more afraid I was of getting fat, the more I had to eat to squelch the fear. I now ate against my will and had lost the power of choice.

For the next eighteen years I was obsessed with food, calories, diets, pills and scales. My food intake determined my mood and my actions. My weight controlled my participation in life. If I binged I couldn't go to school the next day because I would be too sick and bloated. Eventually the "A" average which had represented my only asset fell to a "C" due mainly to absenteeism.

If I binged during the day, I would not go out socially at night because I looked and felt too awful. My social life shrank as my withdrawal from reality progressed. My only pleasures were escapist ones in which I took no active part. Going to movies was my favorite because it was dark, diverting and no one could see how many candy bars I ate.

Reading books about beautiful heroines was another escape, for I lost myself in their adventures. The best escape of all was my fantasy world where I was slim, stunning, charming and every male within a fifty mile radius was pining for me. I pictured in detail my hair, clothes and scintillating personality.

I was a compulsive calorie counter, especially when binging. I would compute over and over how much I had consumed so I could punish myself. I ate to the point of nausea for the same reason. In fact, punishing myself became a fulltime job.

When I was sixteen, I went to work part-time in a drugstore and found another answer: dexamyl. For the next ten years I played Russian roulette with alternating or combined intakes of pills, food and alcohol. I was equally addicted to all three. In this manner I kept my weight under 160 pounds and paid the price in mental, physical and spiritual demoralization.

I lost weight — courtesy of the pills — on special occasions only: when I was "in love," when I became ill with some interesting new malady or when tragedy struck. I welcomed any situation that brought a temporary halt to binging. During a period when I was heavily addicted to diet pills I reached what I thought was the perfect weight for my five feet, seven inches: 95 pounds. My dream of being as scrawny as a Vogue model was finally realized. No more did I have to compare myself with other girls at parties and come out the one with the biggest hips. I felt gorgeous. Never mind such minor drawbacks as anemia and malnutrition.

At this point, two events occurred that caused me to gain 45 pounds in three months: my pill supply was cut off and I got married. My husband had been attracted by my shapely legs and vibrant (chemically induced) personality, both of which rapidly disappeared.

I don't function when I binge. I miss work, get sleepy, depressed and paralyzed. I sat in a chair for eighteen hours, watching television and eating, too scared to open the drapes or answer the telephone. I played the resolution game for years. On Monday or the first of the month or New Year's or my birthday I resolved to go on a diet, stop drinking, not smoke and assume my place in the world.

I was sincere because I neither knew nor would have believed that I was ill and powerless to carry out my resolutions. Resolve, for me, was something that broke down in a matter of hours, leaving me totally bewildered by the repeated failures.

I lost jobs. My husband was a student and we needed the income, but I became too sick to help. I found energy only to get to the market and cause scenes at home. Finally, my husband couldn't take it any more. He left. This prompted a dramatic suicide attempt on my part, followed by two years of therapy.

The earnestness of my efforts to get well lured my husband back home. Soon, he found himself on a treadmill of working, going to school, cooking and cleaning. I felt enormous guilt, but I could not change the destructive course I was on. Therapy was unsuccessful, for I misinterpreted the psychologist's words to fit my needs. I never faced myself or accepted responsibility for my actions. I convinced my husband that as soon as my parent-induced neuroses were cleared up life would be ideal; I would be able to eat and drink moderately. The sad part was that I really believed this. The doctor finally dismissed me.

More compulsive years followed — years of diet doctors, self-help books and resolutions. My husband again decided to leave me. I was desperate. I knew that this decision would be final. I began the OA program only to keep him with me. Before I knew it, I was going to meetings for another reason: a sincere desire to get straightened out. Life, for the first time, held a promise of hope.

The twelve steps introduced me to reality. What a shock it was to discover that I had to assume responsibility for the way I lived, that I was not merely an innocent victim, nor was my illness the fault of cruel parents or a punishing God. I had to become honest with myself and in doing so I was able to let God remove the deadly resentments I had carried against Him, my parents and the world in general. I now had a reason for living. I felt a part of humanity.

After my first month in OA, the compulsion to overeat was removed. I enjoy food now for what it is, not what it used to represent. Food is no longer a weapon with which to get back at "them" or an anesthetic to stupefy my emotions. Working at the twelve steps has slowly filled that big empty hole in my gut which no substance — chemical, refined or 86 proof — could satisfy.

I have been maintaining a 40-pound weight loss for more than a year and a half. It feels strange to be the same size month after month. I used to have clothes in sizes five through sixteen, and alternated up and down with alarming speed. I'll bet I've gained and lost several hundred pounds during my eating years. Now, when I buy a dress, I am fully confident that I'll be able to wear it until *it* shows signs of deterioration, not me.

I have found that if I take my will back and decide that God isn't working quite fast enough, the obsession with food returns. But now I have a choice. I don't have to eat because the program enables me to sit still and hurt. I can now accept emotional pain as a prelude to growth and not try to push it down.

My sponsors and friends truly love me for myself. I don't have to wear false faces or try to impress them. I can be the self I have always longed to be, at home in the world. I'm not on the outside looking in, but rather take an active part in life. I hardly ever go to movies any more. The old escapes just aren't appealing. Helping a newcomer brings every good feeling I looked for in fantasies. Having lost my fear of people, I find I have my own opinions and the courage to express them.

I have even come to like myself, finally. I realize that even at my worst I did the best I could. Guilt has been like a comfortable old shoe and I wear it well. But if God has already forgiven me, it's time for me to forgive myself. Self-worth comes very slowly, but it brings real freedom from all the old ideas.

It has taken a great deal of pain and effort to live in reality. But "we are not saints . . . we are willing to grow along spiritual lines." That sentence has saved me from discouragement many times, for I still insist on taking backward steps. Now that I know a better way, the self-will doesn't last as long. I no longer enjoy suffering.

Recently, I celebrated four years of abstinence from alcohol and two years of abstinence from compulsive overeating. God, as I still don't and maybe never will understand Him, has given me the gift of abstinence and the Fellowship has shown me how to work this beautiful program.

My lifestyle has changed almost in spite of me. I was always a night eater and stayed up late. I slept all day because I hated to wake up to the consequences of my binge and the emptiness of the hours ahead. Now I enjoy getting up early for I have things to do — worthwhile things like going to meetings, keeping a clean house, being a wife and mother. The hours fly by. I have discipline in areas I never imagined I would, such as exercising every morning just because it feels good. I eat more healthfully than ever before. It still amazes me how much energy good natural food provides.

I have learned to be moderate — yes, that scary word — with cigarettes, gum and beverages. I take vitamins instead of drugs, and with all of this clean living, my chronic physical problems have disappeared. I go to bed at a reasonable hour and go right to sleep. No more marathon stomachaches interrupt my nights.

I could never have fantasized a more beautiful life for myself. I want to continue to allow it to happen and keep my destructive self-will out of the way. My hope knows no limits, for God has no limits. I see more growth and freedom. One day at a time, I look forward to a forever in OA.

21

The Overachiever Who Overcame

*D*URING MY SCHOOL YEARS I learned that I could get approval from my parents by being a good girl and doing well academically. I brought home good report cards and my parents were very pleased with my achievement, but I felt an emptiness that only food seemed to fill. My family did not openly display affection, and I longed for the kind of love that I saw expressed with hugs and kisses in other families.

When I realized the impossibility of losing weight, a sort of resignation set in. I accepted what the doctor told me: I would probably lose a day from my life span for every day I overate. Life seemed less worth living, anyway; I didn't care.

After my freshman year in college, I spent a summer in volunteer service at the National Institute of Health in Bethesda, Maryland. As a "normal" control subject in medical research, I requested a moderate diet in the hospital and my weight dropped from 200 pounds to 170 in thirty days. This proved one thing to me: I had no metabolic disorder; I was fat because I ate too much.

I came home thinner than I had ever been in my adult life and told my story of humanitarian service to a college-age church group. The idealistic president of the club was very taken with me and we were married a few months later. I was determined to continue with college and also worked full time until our first child came two and a half years later. I was still in the superachiever syndrome. I overcompensated in the intellectual areas for my painful and overwhelming deficiencies in nearly every other area of my life.

My eating was out of control. I gained weight with both my pregnancies, especially during the six months following delivery. I was totally unable to cope with the housework and we lived in filth and clutter. The children were colicky and drove me up the wall. My husband was progressing down the road of alcoholism, and sex had become very distasteful to me. I went once or twice a week to a family therapist for three years during the early part of our marriage. I appreciated the therapist's love and caring, and I became dependent on her. But I was unable to overcome my sloth, sexual aversion, binge eating and inability to cope with my children.

After eight years, I got my college degree and went to work. It was hard to find a job at 215 pounds, even with my honors in mathematics. I liked to pretend my difficulty was due to discrimination against women, but actually I was uninsurable under many company insurance plans, and some employers had to turn me down. The job I finally got served two main purposes: it kept me from eating for eight hours, since I was a secret eater; and it filled an ego need. I could do well at work and pay someone else to clean my house and take care of the children.

By the time I was twenty-nine, I had eaten my way to 240 pounds and developed the symptoms of diabetes. Again a doctor gave me a frightening talk on the danger to my life and health, and this time I followed his diet to the letter — for a period of five months and a weight loss of 50 pounds. At 190 my diabetic symptoms disappeared, and so did my willpower. Again my eating was out of control and I began vomiting after my binges to keep from regaining the weight.

Realizing the seriousness of trying to control my weight by vomiting, I went to a diet club. I lost 20 pounds in sixteen weeks and received my gold pin while binging on enormous quantities of "free" foods. After that I couldn't limit my binges to the low carbohydrate vegetables. As soon as I had one slice of bread too much, I knew I would eat the whole loaf because it would have to come up anyway. I spent a full year before finding OA binging and regurgitating daily while faithfully attending my diet club meetings and trying all their new recipes, and not losing another pound.

Then, after twelve years of an increasingly rocky marriage, I filed for divorce. In desperation, my husband went to Alcoholics Anonymous and — miracle of miracles — he got sober. I was directed to Al-Anon where I saw firsthand the beautiful changes in family members who practiced AA's twelve steps in their own lives. My husband and I decided to give the marriage another chance.

Strangely, my binging rapidly got worse and my life became even more unmanageable. An Al-Anon friend directed me to OA. She told me that with my compulsion I stood about as much chance of success in Al-Anon as my alcoholic husband would. A compulsive overeater can't fully grasp and develop a spiritual way of life while binging, any more than an alcoholic can while still drinking. To be honest with step three, I could only say I would turn over my will and my life except in the area of food. I read the OA pamphlet with the fifteen questions and I knew without a doubt that I was a compulsive overeater.

I hardly dared hope that OA could solve my various living problems, as it so obviously had for many who spoke at my first meeting. I would be content if only I could stop destroying myself with food. I desperately needed and wanted what those OAs had, so I did as they suggested and took a sponsor the first night. She said, "If you want what I have, do what I did." She had lost 130 pounds by abstaining and diligently following the twelve steps.

I had proved I couldn't do it my way before I came to OA. Now I needed to be open and receptive to the discipline in eating and in the other areas of my life which were suggested in OA. I somehow managed to abstain, one day at a time. I held on to the idea that I just had to postpone eating more until the next mealtime. I read the OA pamphlet, "Before You Take That First Compulsive Bite," with every meal, and I realized that I wanted and needed abstinence more than I wanted and needed food. I quit fighting, and I sensed for the first time in my life a real freedom from the self-destructive urge to overeat.

It was a relief to know that I didn't have to subscribe to any particular belief or faith in order to get on with the steps. I called myself an agnostic, but I knew that the OA group was a power greater than myself, that the twelve steps were a better way to live than I could ever devise, and that God for me was beyond understanding.

Gradually, I became free of the bonds of the past and

willing to try to set right those things that I could. Every day of continued abstinence became an amends to my body for the abuse of overeating in the past. I began to overcome my sloth by doing a number of things every day which I didn't want to do: making my bed, doing the dishes, brushing my teeth and taking a shower. After a time, these tasks became a part of the disciplined way of life which, along with my abstinence, led me to sanity.

The sexual problem in my marriage was overcome as I practiced the third step prayer given in the Big Book of Alcoholics Anonymous. I was released in a large measure from the bondage of self: self-consciousness, self-centeredness and selfishness.

I treated sex in my inventory as suggested in Chapter Five of the Big Book. I came to realize that the most serious offense I committed was the deliberate interference with the development of love and withholding its expression. Overcoming the frigidity in my marriage and clearing away the blocks to the expression of love for my children, family and others were the most profound changes I experienced in OA, aside from the changes in my eating habits.

After eight months of abstinence I had the first of several deeply moving experiences which indicated the presence of a Power that was doing for me what I couldn't do for myself. I began to call that Power God. I had visited a dear OA friend who had broken her long-term abstinence after surgery. She would have given anything to move the clock back. As I drove to work the next morning, I thought of the many who had come to OA before me and after me who were losing their abstinence, and I wondered when it would be my turn, since I was no better than they were. Then it dawned on me that of course I was no better. I was utterly powerless. And yet I had been abstaining for eight months.

How did I do it? I didn't do it. A Power greater than myself whose presence I felt at that moment was doing it through me. I could accept that gift for today. And there was no reason to doubt that the gift of abstinence would continue to be available on a daily basis. Only my self-will, my decision to eat could take it away from me. In acknowledging my true source, I lost my fear and became responsible for myself.

I'm grateful that I have the disease of compulsive overeating, because it turned my life around and transported me to a higher plane. The illness that was killing me is now my chief asset.

22

Something Dependable

*M*Y STORY BEGINS ALMOST twenty-two years ago, when I was born the third of four children. My father was a doctor, and ours was what is looked upon as a respectable, secure family. There was always plenty of food, snacking being a favorite pastime with all of us. Who would imagine that the good times we had over food might be dangerous, that the coziness of gathering at my parents' bed to share a nighttime candy bar might be awakening in a seven-year-old an insatiable appetite for sugar that would take control of her whole life?

Yet the problem was already apparent then. I alone among the children would make my way back to my parents' bedroom to rifle through my mother's drawers for more candy. My mother was learning fast that she had to hide food from me, and learning almost as fast that hiding it didn't do much good.

Looking back, this was the first indication that I was powerless over food. I never planned to eat everybody else's share; the humiliation it caused me was great. Yet once I began eating, my judgment vanished and I could not stop.

In my first two years of high school I dieted successfully, but to do so I became totally self-centered and bitter. I was vicious to my parents, blaming them for my misery. Waves of self-pity came over me that I should have to deprive myself of everything to stay thin. As I saw it, my life was certainly a hard one, and I wanted it to end whenever my body seemed out of control.

What control I had fell apart soon enough. I gained 35 pounds in a few months. It was a time when I was beginning to care about others and the problems of humanity. I didn't know how to care about myself. I hated myself. Embarrassed to be seen, I stayed in my room as much as possible, feeling sorry for the world and sorry that all my sensitivity had to turn up as fat on my body. Again I imposed on family, this time by isolating myself from their projects, refusing to wear attractive clothes (I didn't even put on a swimsuit for two years), and talking constantly about the diet I never went on.

The awareness that nobody believed me, that I couldn't believe myself, poisoned my self-esteem. I began to feel that nothing I tried would ever work out because I was too untalented and undisciplined. In an effort to show everyone (myself, especially) that maybe I wasn't so bad, I crash-dieted while traveling for a few months. I came back 40 pounds thinner, eager to start college as an attractive young lady, a perfect daughter. A frightening episode interfered with my plans. At dinner my first night home I experienced a feeling of no control; the world seemed to be spinning around me and I didn't know how to handle it. That evening, I began compulsively overeating on a new scale.

I panicked at the thought of being fat and miserable again. I began to make myself vomit after really bad binges, each time swearing I would never do it again. Throwing up was painful physically and emotionally, but the fact that food no longer made me fat rendered it that much more attractive. I wanted it so badly, had always longed for it; now there was nothing to keep me from eating all I wanted.

The five years that followed, during which I became progressively enslaved to my compulsion, taught me that no amount of food would ever be enough for me. I lied to everyone about how much I ate. My mother developed a guilt complex because I told her I only overate at home. I didn't worry about her feelings. I just had to make sure she didn't find out how insane my eating really was. She never knew that under my bed were bags of garbage from food I carried around in my bookbag.

My greatest heartache was that I expected myself to make great strides in academia, yet my work was not very good. How could it be when I spent ten or more hours a day eating? I thought something must be holding me back from using my willpower and I sought help from two psychiatrists. I asked one, in a deadpan manner, whether I was weak. I was afraid he would say yes, but he didn't. In fact, he helped me to see the good in myself. Both doctors seemed to think that I would give up overeating when I no longer needed it. But when that day would come, I had no idea. Willpower still seemed to be the answer, and I didn't think I had any. I had been looking for an easier way in therapy. When I didn't find it, I stopped going.

Soon after graduation from college, I developed infectious mononucleosis. Bedridden for six weeks, I went on another food rampage as soon as I could get up. It was worse than ever. I moved into my own apartment to avoid the stimulation of my roommate's food. That was another joke. The only thing living alone did for me was remove the stigma of having my eating habits known. I now cooked and ate regularly until five o'clock in the morning, then tried to function that day. The inside of my mouth was full of canker sores and burns from biting myself and not waiting for food to cool. I was spending thirty dollars a day on food when I didn't steal it from the restaurant where I worked. (Everyone else stole, didn't they?) My purse was like a garbage can full of wrappers because I couldn't go anywhere without things to nibble on.

I had never given my body a rest after the mono, so quite naturally my exertions were now driving me to my bed every two weeks with another cold and fever. My mother was alarmed, as was my doctor, when my health never improved. I knew why it didn't, but I could hardly tell them that incessant eating and vomiting were responsible for my condition.

It was then that my mother showed me an article about OA. She was beginning to suspect that my overeating was a drain on my health, though she didn't know about the vomiting. In any event, I saw myself in the description of the compulsive overeater.

I went to my first meeting that week. I was ecstatic! I wanted to cry or scream with relief at the honesty I heard. These people spoke my language.

My hope was to be able to stop overeating and start living up to my high moral standards without accepting God. I was agnostic. In time, the force of good became my Higher Power, but this had one vital shortcoming: I couldn't ask it for help. I continued to flounder through life and food alone, until I read the

AA book, *Came to Believe*. It proved to be the most valuable book I have ever read. It taught me to pray. It showed me that I didn't have to be able to justify my Higher Power intellectually; I just had to depend upon it, and the sooner I stopped worrying that faith in something greater than myself was stupid and weak, the sooner relief would come.

I was lucky enough to find people who needed to hear my story because they were also caught in the snare of vomiting. It was only in having my experience be of use to others that I finally was able to forgive myself. Through feeling their pain, I was able to ache for myself after so many years of pretending that the problem wasn't me.

Food has become the least important part of my program. I never thought I would be able to say that. Today, if I am living my life right, I do not overeat. I must add that I don't view abstinence as something I go on and off. If I did, I would have to say that I go on and off living, because today for me to binge is to die. It is to shut out of my life everything I believe in. It is to be dishonest and pretend that I can stop eating without turning my life over to a Higher Power when I know I cannot. It is to pretend that there is no Higher Power than myself, when I know there is, or that there is no beautiful world to live in, when I have already found one.

23

The Minister's Daughter

*F*OR MANY YEARS I WAS unhappy, overweight, depressed, prone to headaches and backaches, snappy with my children, sulky with my husband and certain that I had no friends I could call "good friends."

Today, I am at a good weight, healthy, positive about the future, certain that I made the best possible choice of husbands, proud of my children and blessed with many good friends, including several who are very special. The twelve-step program has made the difference in my life. The simple, no-nonsense approach to living which I have acquired through the Fellowship of Overeaters Anonymous has given me a life that is beautiful, fun, exciting and spiritually satisfying.

I was raised in a loving and happy home. My father is a retired Baptist minister, well-loved and respected by many. During his years as a church pastor, I was proud of being the minister's daughter. Somehow I knew, even then, that I had been blessed. Some of my friends were poorly treated, severely punished for seemingly inconsequential reasons; I had no such complaints. My parents were fair, honest and open, and they disciplined us by allowing us to suffer the consequences of our own deeds.

I am the oldest of three children. I got along well in school; I wasn't the smartest but I held my own in classes and I enjoyed school. After high school, my parents felt that I was too young for college, so I worked for a year while living at home, and then attended drama school in Chicago for a year. Eventually, I did go to college, graduating with a degree in psychology and education and a teaching certificate. I worked for two years as secretary to a psychologist at a large university, testing college students and helping with research papers.

I married the boy I had dated since high school and taught kindergarten for four years before leaving to await the birth of our first child. Five and one half years later, I had four children and 60 extra pounds. What difference did it make? I was home with the children where I wanted to be, and I didn't need to be thin anymore. It was obvious to me that God planned for me to be a large woman and anyway, I really didn't care that much.

As the children grew older and didn't need the minute-to-minute care, I began to look at myself more closely. I didn't like what I saw. I didn't like the way I felt, either. The headaches were a recurring event, lasting from twenty-four to thirty-six hours and making me unbearable to live with. My night-eating syndrome was both sneaky and scary: I would outwait my husband every night, knowing that his going to bed was an invitation for me to start eating. I knew this was wrong, but I was on a relentless treadmill and I didn't know how to get off.

I went to my first Overeaters Anonymous meeting as soon as I was back on my feet after a thrombophlebitis convalescence. I had a chip on my shoulder: "It won't work. Nothing ever did." I was convinced that one meeting would be enough to show me what it was all about. I had tried two popular weight-losing clubs and just about every diet printed.

I found that fat was not my only problem. For many years, I felt I was not capable of doing anything right. I stayed away from groups that seemed to be close and sharing with the excuse that I was busy with the children and didn't have time for such nonsense. I never visited in others' homes; I might "bother" them. Others never visited my home; what's the matter, did they need an invitation?

I was not willing to do the footwork that is needed to have a good friend. If people did not come to me with open arms, I could not handle the risk involved in going to them.

The twelve-step program pulled out all the props under these problems. It has let me see that I was living a self-centered, self-defeating life.

My first six months in OA involved a diet, pure and simple. I have since accepted the fact that I had to handle the physical side of this program first. It was important to me to get those pounds off, to feel good physically. It was not a good abstinence as such, for when the weight was almost all off I began to think to myself, "There, I've got this thing licked; OA is really great, it helped me lose and now I'm normal again."

A painful year of progressive relapse followed. After I had regained about half the weight, I realized that my experience did not make me a failure. Nor was the program a failure. I got out the Big Book and really read it. I committed myself to abstinence; yes, that was the right way to say it. I decided what my abstinence would be, and I committed myself to eating (and not eating) by that plan.

I also committed myself to study and service — and to the twelve steps. The pattern for living that they set is so remarkable that I am constantly amazed by the wisdom of the people who formed them. There is a logical progression from acceptance to surrender to action; from clearing away the past to building daily practices for the future; from learning what the message is myself to being willing to share that message with others.

I was brought up in a minister's home, but it took OA to show me how to turn my life and my will over to the care of God on a daily basis. I was ready for Overeaters Anonymous and when it came to me I opened my soul and mind to it. I lost the weight and gained peace and serenity. I lost my depressions and gained the expectancy of each new day. I lost my feeling that I had no friends, for I gained a nationwide Fellowship of "instant" friends and many close, special friends as well as a sponsor who knows me inside and out and loves me anyway!

24

The Atheist Who Made a Zif

A COMPULSIVE OVEREATER, THEY SAY, is a sort
of guilt detector. If there's any guilt
around, you pick it up, take it home, nurture it, feed it,
love it.

I felt guilty as a kid because I used to have nightmares all the time. They were always the same. Some
devil or monster was chasing me and I'd wake up
screaming. This happened when I was about ten years
old. In that same year, I figured out a way to get rid of
these dreams. I became an atheist. Since there was no
God, he wasn't going to send devils or monsters after
me.

I stopped having the nightmares. I would say, "Go
ahead, throw a lightning bolt at me. I know you're not
there. It's all those weak people who need to believe in
God. Me, I'm strong. I don't need you."

What I did need was to eat and eat. At thirteen, when all the other boys were starting to go out with girls, I weighed 200 pounds. My parents took me to a doctor who gave me thyroid, which was what they used before speed was invented. When I was twenty, they found another doctor. This one put me on a "modified fast" diet. I ate nothing for two weeks at a time. This had a profound effect on me because I soon discovered that breaking such a long fast made me vomit. My stomach couldn't tolerate the food. But if I stopped every five or ten minutes on the way home, I could eat for seventy-two hours straight. That really sharpened my ability to binge.

In spite of the binging, however, I lost about 82 pounds that summer. I was down to a trim 217. It was the first time in my life that I could walk into a real people's store instead of a fat men's store where you pay twice as much for styles that went out thirty years ago. The suit I bought was olive green. I felt so good when I tried it on and it fit. It was the biggest size they had in the store, but it was a "regular" store and the suit fit.

I went back to school and decided it was time to start going out. I had never been on a date in my life. I took one girl out and the highlight of the evening was when she got out of the car. I thought, "Thank God, that's over with." I had been very uncomfortable. I didn't know what to do or say. I forced myself to try it again and it was the same: the best part of the evening was when the girl left.

At that time I was living with three roommates. One of them introduced me to a friend of a friend, a girl who was also "people." She used to come over and we'd talk. I started going out with her. We went together for about two months and finally, at twenty-one, I had sex for the first time. We got married in June. I weighed

297 pounds. I hadn't had a chance to wear that olive green suit a half dozen times before it didn't fit any more. I certainly didn't wear it at my wedding; it wouldn't have fit on one leg.

We moved to California and my life took on some really exciting aspects. I would have a giant breakfast, then go to work. At about 9:30 the coffee shop downstairs would send up "refreshments" for the coffee break. I always had a couple. First, though, I'd sneak downstairs and have a few early ones, and after the coffee break I'd go back down and finish off what was left. Around noon, the catering truck came and I'd have a big lunch, then eat some more at the afternoon coffee break. And always, on the way home from work, I had to stop for something to eat. In the evening, after a big dinner, I would lie on the couch and watch television while my wife fed me sugar. Each night I faded into a stupor and then got up the next morning and started again.

That was the way I maintained 325 pounds. One day I walked into a drugstore and noticed a little diet book. I bought it and counted my calories for about nine months. I lost 120 pounds. Now came the ego. You see, I had always thought I was great, even when my self-worth was nonexistent. I could never admit that I was wrong. I made up "facts" to win an argument. Now, having lost that weight, I *knew* I was great. For one thing, when I was fat it was clear to me that I was crazy: one look told me that. But when I lost the weight, I thought I was sane because I believed it was the fat that had been making me crazy.

There's nothing more dangerous than a crazy person who thinks he's sane. I got divorced. Then I went on a spree to try to make up for all the fun I had missed. I was "going steady" with three women at the same time once, and my roommate had a list of who to tell what when they called.

I have a theory that if a person has a fat head and a thin body, one has to catch up with the other. I maintained my weight for a while with "sensible" eating techniques such as nothing but carrots for a week. Or all the celery you can eat with nothing in between. For binging between fasts, laxatives were my bag. The only problem was they didn't work; I ate again as soon as I had that nice empty feeling.

Slowly, the weight started to creep up. During this second thin period, I had taken up sports. I was the fellow whose worst subject in school was gym. I would wash the coach's car, clean his desk, do anything I had to do to get out of gym. I couldn't do a single sit-up or pushup; I couldn't run thirty feet. My body was a total handicap. Now, when I lost all that weight and started surfing and playing volleyball and water skiing, it was as if I had been a quadriplegic all my life and suddenly I had full use of my limbs. My body was functioning. My body could bring me joy. It was a wonderful feeling.

But I started to gain the weight back. First slowly, then faster. I was losing my body again. There wasn't a water ski big enough to float me anymore; and snow skiing, I looked like an avalanche rolling down the hill. Nobody would play volleyball with me. I had an eleven-foot surfboard and I couldn't get out of the water on it. I had one girlfriend left and the relationship was very tenuous. At work, where I held a technical sales position, my bosses were telling me that I was not a fit representative for the company.

One night, I lay on my bed with a pain in my chest. I knew what it was. The doctors had all promised me a heart attack by the time I was thirty. All my life I knew that was what I was going to get for my birthday unless I lost weight. In the morning, I walked across the street to the emergency room of the hospital and checked myself in. They ran an EKG, and when the orderly came out later I asked, "What is it?" He told me it was "pudgy pain."

I was an atheist; I couldn't make a solemn oath to God, but I made one to myself. This was it. I had dieted before and I was going to do it again. It was the shortest diet I was ever on. It lasted four lanes. I walked back across the street and ate sugar for about four hours. Then I went on a diet and lost 35 pounds in eight weeks, and after that I went on another diet and lost 25 pounds in six weeks. I always gained back that weight with a little bonus — five or ten pounds for trying.

The night I hit bottom is very clear in my memory. My roommate was home. This guy was the greatest ladies' man in all of Southern California. He would go out to a bar or someplace and come home with a beautiful woman every night. That night he had come in with a girl and I could hear them talking upstairs. I was sitting on my bed with my package of goodies next to me, eating and crying. I thought, "There's no sense trying to quit eating because I can't. For some reason I'm different from other people. The only choice I have is to just enjoy my food. I'm going to lose my job, and I'm going to die, but hopefully when I go it'll be fast; I won't have to be an invalid."

I had never heard of the twelve steps and I knew nothing about Alcoholics Anonymous, but that night I took step one. I admitted that I was powerless over food and my life was unmanageable, right at gut level. And I also took step three, in a way. I made a decision right then and there to turn my will and my life over to my higher power, which was food. But it was a good start. It set the stage.

At this time, I was being treated by my doctor for dysentery. That good man had been delighted to see me lose weight and now he was horrified that I was gaining it all back. The dysentery I was suffering was so severe I would almost pass out. Yet I gained 14 pounds in one month. We didn't know what caused the dysentery until after I got into Overeaters Anonymous. It was from pouring sugar into myself at such a rate that my system wouldn't tolerate it.

On one visit, the doctor ran an EKG and a heart vector. He told me things were not good. "You can't afford to gain any more weight," he said. "You have to lose it or you're going to die."

"I know that," I said, "but don't bother to give me a diet because it's a waste of your paper."

"When you go outside," he said, "I want you to ask my secretary for the OA phone number. I have a patient who is a member and she said to have people like you call her."

A woman answered the phone. "I want you to tell me all there is to know about this Overeaters Anonymous," I told her.

"I can't do that," she said. "It's too complicated to explain."

I really believe that God put this woman there because if she had tried to tell me what Overeaters Anonymous was about, I would have said, "Phtt," and gone out and died. Instead, I went to a meeting. I sat in the back row behind a post. Two large women sat down on either side of me. I couldn't get out.

When the meeting started, the first thing I heard was "God." I thought, Hah! Now I know. The next thing, they're going to want to convert me and they're going to bless me and dip me in water. I see what the gimmick is now.

When they called the coffee break, I saw my chance. I got up and started to leave. But people flocked around me and started talking to me. It seemed I was the only newcomer there. Before I could escape, the meeting started again. The speaker started off by saying, "I used to be 325 pounds and I'm now 180 pounds and my goal is to be half the man I once was."

I thought, "Uh-huh." Then he passed his picture around and it didn't look as though it was touched up. It was a real snapshot. I didn't hear anything else that night, but after the meeting I had to talk to that man. I had to know the secret. I had to make sure he was real. He invited me to go to coffee with the group.

"No, I can't," I said. "I'm busy. Winchell's will close in three hours."

But they kept asking me and it appeared obvious that they really wanted me. No one had wanted me for anything in so long that I went.

At home, I began thinking: The speaker was thin and she used to be fat, too. Maybe I'd better get a sponsor. I realized that I had only one telephone number: the woman I had first talked with. When I called and asked her to be my sponsor, she said, "I'd love to."

I called her every day for five months and I got to love that lady. She was about sixty-two years old and six-foot, three-inches tall, and she talked like a truck-driver. I didn't try to con her, ever. She said, "Do it," and I did it.

My Higher Power began evolving the day I heard someone suggest that nonbelievers make "a zif." I was an atheist; not an agnostic. An agnostic has doubts. I had never doubted anything. I knew there was no God. When I learned that "a zif" meant "acting as if," I was told that I didn't have to believe in anything. All I had to do was say, "God, I don't believe you're there, but anyway, I'd like such and such."

"You're asking me to be a hypocrite," I said.

"Oh, heaven forbid! You could be a glutton, a thief and an egomaniac — vicious in every possible way; you could smell bad, you could look bad, but by God, we don't want you to be a hypocrite!"

I said, "OK, I'll try it."

At first my Higher Power looked like my sponsor. Then he looked like me. Then, like a kind old man with a big beard. My Higher Power has always been a loving Higher Power. My sponsor told me, "You can choose anything you want, but it's got to be benevolent, not malevolent." So I started to develop a Higher Power that was sort of a spirit of the universe, and if I was in touch with that flow then I would go the easy way and good things would happen. And they did. Things just happened, one right after another. Beautiful things.

One morning I was eating breakfast and reading my twenty-four hour book when there was an earthquake. The house was rocking back and forth, and I felt a great rush of warmth several times. It was as if God was in me. He was rocking me back and forth in His arms and I was smiling. Nobody smiles during an earthquake. I sat there at the table and I picked up the twenty-four hour book and opened it and it said, "Fear not fire or earthquake." A cold chill shot through me and I went upstairs and took a shower with one eye open, thinking, "God, please don't be standing there when I get out of this shower because I'll die. You're not supposed to be there."

It got so I was praying for parking places and getting them.

About nine months ago, I was standing in my kitchen and I felt the warm flash again. I'm happy to say it's back. I have a good conscious contact with my Higher Power. We talk to each other. He knows I'm a screw-up, that I do things wrong. But He doesn't mind. He loves me pure and true, as only a perfect being can love. I can't love you that way, and you can't love me that way because we're not perfect. Only He can love us that way.

25

Whatever It Takes, I'll Do

I ALWAYS KNEW THERE was something wrong with me. My weight problem started when I was twelve, but I had always been a very unhappy child. I have a vivid picture of myself standing in a corner, crying. Communicating my feelings was difficult. Consequently, it was hard to make friends. I knew everybody hated me.

I left home when I was nineteen and moved in with a girl who was extremely overweight. I disliked her immediately; fat people appalled me. My own battle with weight had left me resentful of this condition. As a teenager, I had tried every diet ever invented. My mother brought all of them to my attention and I followed them just to make her happy. Each diet lasted about two days. I was promised new wardrobes, money and, one time, anything I wanted — to no avail.

Immature and naive for my age, at twenty I knew nothing about boy/girl relationships and what they entailed. I met and married a man who was very thin and who accepted me the way I was and gave me the attention I needed. I had no understanding of what was expected of me as a wife. After our marriage, I hated sex and avoided it as often as possible by staying up late watching television and eating. When I did give in it was because I felt it was my duty.

I did as little work around the house as possible. When the neighbors got together for coffee, I would just sit and listen. I still couldn't communicate my feelings. Besides, I was so naive I often didn't know what they were talking about. I felt I scored points by letting them know I was a very good listener.

My husband never complained about my weight, possibly because I never allowed him to see just how much I ate. I hid in the kitchen, "cleaning up" — a process that consisted primarily of eating the leftovers.

No matter how much I was given — new house, new car, new furniture — or how much money my husband made, it was never enough to make me happy. Through two pregnancies my attention and energies were focused on eating and dieting, gaining weight and losing it. In between there were diet pills and depression. Wanting badly to be liked, I would bend over backward to do things for people, hating what I was doing and despising myself for doing it. I thought of suicide many times, but I was afraid I would bungle the job and lie there in pain.

One day, a friend who weighed more than 300 pounds asked me to attend a new weight meeting with her. I agreed to go just to keep her company. When I walked in the door to my first OA meeting I was so "ready" that had they told me to crawl on the floor I would have done it. Imagine finding out that there were other people who had the same problem I did and that there was a name for it!

They said all you have to do is live one day at a time. I didn't have to worry about my past anymore — childhood, parents, any of it. Or my future, either. Next morning, I turned off the television, switched on the radio and started singing. My family thought I had flipped. I opened my curtains and looked out and said, "To hell with trying to please everyone! I don't need that anymore!"

I began losing weight — 50 pounds in two months. My neighbors started coming around and for the first time I enjoyed their company.

The following month I attended an OA convention where I met the person who was to be my first sponsor. He asked if I had worked the steps and I said No, they hadn't been explained that well.

He said, "How about if I come to your meeting and bring some people with me who can do just that?"

He came with two women a week later. That was the beginning of the changes that were to come in my life. With my fourth step, I got rid of all my hangups from childhood — hatred for parents, jealousies, uncomfortable feelings about sex and many other aspects of life. I felt my face clearing up for the first time in my life. There were no longer frown marks on my forehead. Where there had been drooping lines of depression there was now a wide smile. It felt like liquid draining out of my face. I wanted to tell everyone about this miracle, so I started speaking to various groups in the area.

The years that followed were not without their problems. This program is not a once-in-a-while thing. It is an everyday commitment. The abstinence is for the fat downstairs and the twelve steps are for the fat upstairs — in the head.

After finally attaining a normal weight I decided to go to work. Now the compliments started coming. Being admired was a new experience and I enjoyed it. I had never been thin since early childhood and I had never had so much attention from the opposite sex. It was too much to handle. I got involved with a man at work. At this point, my second sponsor turned up, helping me through many tenth steps and even an attempt to kill myself after the affair ended.

I thought I was beginning to grow up, so it was a shock when, during a third pregnancy, I gained my weight back. I had never expected this, though I realized that I had let go of my program. It was not easy to begin again, but with two months of abstinence, my weight was almost back to normal.

After living for a year in a small town that had no OA meetings, we moved to a large city where I continued to lose weight. Then my husband began losing jobs again. Out of insecurity, I starting eating and the weight crept back on. I prayed and attended meetings regularly, but my mind was not open and I didn't hear anything. In spite of my pain, however, I knew my Higher Power was listening and would eventually allow me to lose the weight when I was ready.

Two years ago, I worked part-time for an agency that sent me to a job where another OA member was employed. She was abstaining and she talked program every day. I didn't always listen, but I heard. After I left that job, I continued talking to her on the telephone. Finally, it got through to me. I started abstaining. Again, I lost all my excess weight. I had reached my last bottom.

Abstinence for me now is not eating any of my binge foods. But that is not my problem. I am my problem. I have to read my literature, practice my steps and let go of my will every morning. I can never again forget who

I am or where I came from. I call an OA member every morning, even if it is just to say Good morning. This is part of my program. Whatever it takes to keep this weight off and the peace of mind I now have is what I will do. If it means making phone calls by the dozen and going to two and three meetings a week, I do it. Helping others, speaking at meetings, spreading the word. This time I am desperate and I will go to any lengths to keep my program. It is a constant daily program of reading, phoning and working with others.

The beauty we all share comes from within and if we don't have that, no matter how much weight we lose, we have nothing. Giving service, working the steps and abstaining one day at a time — these are the tools for this wonderful program for living.

26

Indian Summer

*L*OVE AND FEAR HAVE BEEN at war in me since I can first remember.

I was the baby of the family. To me, this meant that father, mother, grandmother, three older brothers and a big sister were all there to tell me what to do. If I tried to participate in family affairs, someone was sure to tell me to sit down, be quiet, don't show off because you don't know anything about it.

I believed them.

My parents thought that praise made children vain. Good grades in school were noted without comment. When I won a spelling contest, strangers congratulated me, but at home nothing was said. I concluded that my family did not care, that to them I was still stupid.

No one deliberately taught me these things. They are

what I learned.

My older sister, who was twice my size, dominated me completely. She was fat, poor child, and she passed her discontent on to me by convincing me that I was not only stupid but ugly. She ordered me to wait on her like a little slave. If I protested, my mother always made me surrender because she dreaded her older daughter's explosive temper. She would then try to make it up to me with hugs and kisses.

I loved and resented my mother. But I never doubted her love for me. It was the sun that warmed my days, my shelter in storms.

My father always made me feel unnecessary, a tagalong. It seemed that all his tenderness was taken up by my sister, the first girl after three boys. He appeared to notice me only to reprimand me or to take something away from me.

Young as I was, I sensed my father's integrity. It was at odds with his treatment of me, but it validated my inferiority.

We were raised in a very straitlaced kind of religion. Everything pleasurable was suspect. Hell awaited the poor sinner who dabbled in "joys of the flesh." I knew all about hell, having listened to many a vivid description by shouting evangelists. I knew it was my destination because I was so bad.

Meek, mousy child, how did that heavy conviction of my "badness" enter my heart? Was it because I could never hope to meet the standards set for some impossible angel-child? Or was it because of thoughts I dared not express? Whatever the cause, the guilt, fear and unworthiness stayed with me.

When did I learn to be an overeater? I was a scrawny child, though we lived on a farm and food was plentiful. I remember looking at a favorite food on my plate and leaving it because I had enough.

As I approached adolescence, we left the farm and moved to town where my father opened a small business. He worked hard but those were Depression years and he didn't have a chance. From plenty of food we fell to scarcity. As a consequence, I grew even thinner and anemic. I had frequent bouts with bronchitis. Is this when I learned to worship food?

I was painfully shy, and though my grades were excellent, I still thought of myself as stupid and bad. After one year at the local college, I boarded a bus with a little cardboard suitcase containing all I owned and headed for the nearest city to find work.

In the year that followed I had seven different jobs. And I fell in love. John was a soldier. We were akin, two people who belonged together. He saw me as beautiful and brave; for him, I began to be what he thought me. I bloomed.

Children of the Depression, we could not afford to marry and have a family. So we waited. I made a bargain with God: We would be "good" — no premarital sex — and God would see that we had a life together.

As U.S. involvement in World War II approached, my fears for John grew. He had been sent to San Francisco for special training. I joined him and we were married. We had two weeks together. Then he was shipped to the Philippines.

I was alone in a strange city, with no friends and a crushing load of anxiety. I began eating. My weight rose to 200 pounds before I knew what was happening. I was appalled. I quickly dieted down to 140 pounds for John's sake. It was not hard.

No sooner had I lost the weight, however, when I became ill. I had fever, nausea and pain. The doctors could not determine what was wrong. I was hospitalized and put under observation. After two weeks I told them to operate or send me home. They operated and removed a perfectly healthy appendix.

I was doing defense work when the wire came: John was dead. He was captured on Bataan, went through the infamous death march and died six months later of fever and starvation.

I plunged into a bottomless rage at God. Though I had never regarded Him as loving, I had thought Him just. Now I knew better. In my anger and grief, I shut everyone out. I carried that anger and grief for thirty years.

I do not condemn myself now for the brief period of promiscuity that followed. In my heartbroken loneliness, I looked for something, anything to hold to, even for a little while. When I found myself pregnant, I had no thought of asking help from anyone. I was fiercely determined to keep my baby and give it all my love.

I had been corresponding with a lonely soldier overseas. He was back now, and he wanted to marry me, baby and all. I did not love him, but I accepted him. He needed me, and I needed some kind of life, I thought.

I lost that first baby. Two years later I had two others, little boys, and the realization that I had married an alcoholic.

The Big Book of AA speaks of self-interest that places us in a position to be hurt. I knew that our marriage could never be what I hoped for, but I feared that if I left my husband I could not support my children. So I stayed, out of fear and self-interest, and I was in a position to be hurt.

When the youngsters were four and five, we had a third son. Little Johnny was a beautiful, sunny baby, a delight to both of us. But when he was a year old he developed a mysterious illness and after some weeks we had to take him to the hospital where he was given blood transfusions. Then he was sent home, much improved. I sat holding my dear little one on my lap and watched my two older children at play. A feeling of thankfulness welled up in me. For the first time since John's death, I spoke to God: "Thank you for my sons."

Johnny died of leukemia soon afterward.

Once again, I closed the door on God. "You've hurt me enough. Let me alone. Forget I'm here."

What did I have left? Two little boys. They became my only reason for existing, and I tried to live my life through them. What a burden I put on them!

My husband's drinking got worse and so did my own disease. My weight climbed past 300 pounds. From time to time I dieted and lost weight. But a terrible craving would begin gnawing at me day and night. Soon, all determination and hope were gone, along with the dieting and the weight loss.

Predictably, the children were not thriving emotionally. Our older son was a quiet, well-behaved boy, very bright in school but withdrawn and unhappy. When he reached puberty, he began to put on excess weight. I watched him become fatter and more detached as he went through high school, but I knew no way to help him. I couldn't help myself.

Our younger child was a funloving, outgoing boy, a favorite of sorts with his father. But he got into a minor scrape at twelve, and his father never let him forget it. Time after time, my husband drove the boy out of the house at the slightest provocation. Eventually he married and moved away, which relieved some of the strain.

Our older son attended college for one year, during which he made the dean's list. The next year he flunked out due to lack of interest. He got a job working evenings. When he came home he would stay up all night reading, eating and watching television. He slept all day and got up in time to go to work. That was his life at twenty-four.

I was now fifty-six. I weighed more than 300 pounds. My feet and ankles swelled hugely; I had arthritis in my knees. My blood pressure was at stroke level.

"But my general health is good," I told the doctor.

"You are very sick," said the doctor. "This can kill you. You must lose weight."

I thought it was nice of her to care, but I didn't. Why should I? All I had to look forward to was my husband's retirement in a year, when he would be home all the time, drinking. I had never driven a car, and my husband never took me anywhere. I could not walk a block without becoming winded. I knew that I could never hope for any escape, any pleasure in life except the food with which I sedated myself. My life was over. I was just marking time, waiting for the hearse.

Then one day my obese older son, who had his mother's compulsion, went to an OA meeting. He came home with all the little pamphlets. I observed his enthusiasm with doubt: Would he stay with it or give up after awhile? Loving mother that I am, I figured that if I started this OA thing with my son, it would help him to continue.

So I went to my first meeting. I was wearing my one dress, a homemade cotton print that I had enlarged from the biggest pattern I could find. And I had two front teeth missing; when you weigh 300 pounds, who cares about your teeth?

All I heard that night was weight loss, "get a sponsor" and "keep coming back." It was enough. I got a sponsor, and I kept coming back.

Abstinence was easy. I did not question the why or how, but for the first time I had something that limited my food and, unaccountably, kept me comfortable. I was hungry by mealtime, of course — probably the first real hunger I had felt for years.

I was quite satisfied with this until I began hearing

something else at meetings: the twelve-step program. I wanted no part of that, thank you. I had no desire for a spiritual life, and as for turning anything over to the likes of the Higher Power I had known — impossible! But they told me that if I did not follow the steps I would not keep my abstinence. I had tasted hope and I could not give it up. So I did as I was told as best I could. My recovery began.

Through my shell of bitterness and hopelessness, the therapy of love reached me. Delicate green tendrils took root in the big aching hollow inside me that food could never fill. As my weight dropped, OA friends rejoiced with me.

With gentle but relentless prodding, people called on me to lead meetings, even to speak at other meetings. From the start, I said yes instead of no. I had let fear speak for me long enough; I couldn't live with it anymore. Soon the old shyness and fear of people were gone. I was at last free to be myself.

The practicing alcoholic who was my husband now had a new problem. He had been accustomed to a wife who was a doormat, a martyr mother. Without quite knowing what had happened, he found himself confronted by a stranger who said things like, "I think I'll get a wig," and "I'm going to the dentist." The men he worked with razzed him: "She's wearing makeup and getting her hair done? And she stays out late and you don't know where she is? Uh-oh!" Funny they should guess that I was running away from home, one meeting at a time.

Though none of us knew it, my husband was mortally ill. He died a few weeks before he was due to retire. We were able to accept the sad reality of his life and death with compassion: "He loved us as much as he could. He did his best." There was a sense of peace, a release from pain, and that was all.

Abstinence, weight loss and personal growth do not solve all of life's difficulties. The last two years have been especially trying as I sought solutions to my own and my troubled younger son's problems. But great progress has been made. My older son, for whose sake I came to OA, lost all his excess weight in the first seven months. Now happily married, he has been maintaining the loss for six years.

Throughout the bad times and the good, the love and assistance of OA friends has been there, sustaining me. I am rich in friendship, who once was so destitute. At an age when too many women are living in the past, I am privileged to be growing, learning, sharing in life. Best of all, I am living at peace with God.

In my springtime years I met with disaster: Depression, war and tragic loss. In my summer years I propped up an alcoholic in his sickness and my own. But this is my Indian Summer, my golden autumn. I am glad to be fully alive every day of it.

27

Beyond Affliction

So GREAT HAD BEEN MY isolation before coming to OA that not once had I ever told anyone about my binging, not even the psychiatrist who treated me for severe depression.

But even in OA it took me a long time to be able to admit that I was a compulsive overeater — even to myself. For nearly one year I remained a "half measure" member, playing around with abstinence, still convinced that my weight was my only problem. I balked at everything from finger salad to God, sure that I was smarter than all that, still in control. And then something unexpected happened that taught me a hard lesson in powerlessness and changed my life.

At the age of twenty-two, almost overnight, I was stricken with a disease that took away ninety percent of my eyesight and left me legally blind, with little hope for any future return of vision. The doctors gave me an apologetic, "There's nothing more we can do," and released me to pursue on my own the channels of state and federal support for the blind.

Understandably, I became despondent and withdrawn. Unfortunately, I also withdrew from OA, which of course led to a resumption of uncontrolled eating. The binging progressed in severity, eventually resulting in a violent case of food poisoning. The effect of this illness on my morale was devastating. I hit an emotional bottom lower than I had ever imagined possible.

For a while I thought I was going to die and, indeed, I wondered if that wouldn't be the best solution to my problems. I was so scared, and so sick. But lying there that night, trembling and crying, I started to pray — to whom or what I didn't know. Presently, I became aware of something deep within me that didn't want to die, that wanted desperately to live and be free. I continued to pray not to die, to be given another chance.

I know now that this prayer was answered by a God I didn't even believe in at the time, for somehow I found my way back to OA. There, the friends I had made were waiting with open arms and hearts. They took me to meetings, read literature to me, and literally held my hand through days when that was all that would help.

One member had me come and live with her for a while, where she lovingly prepared three abstinent meals each day. Another recorded a fourth-step inventory guide on a cassette tape so that I could continue with that important part of the program.

I attended meetings daily and was in the constant company of other OA members. This not only helped keep me abstinent, but it greatly eased the adjustment to my blindness. But most importantly, as I look back now, I was persuaded, despite my fears, to attend my first OA retreat. There, I received the spiritual counsel from the retreat master to allow myself to feel and ac-knowledge my grief, and to be honest enough to tell God that I was angry and felt deserted by Him.

This I did with a vengeance, letting out in one after-noon alone in my room years of suppressed hatred for a God I unconsciously blamed for all the unhappiness of my life. To my surprise, when I was through I felt strangely cleansed and relieved of the burden of "God-pleasing" under which I had lived all my life. I had destroyed the fearsome, cruel God of my own mak-ing, and was open at last to the discovery of a new God who could be my friend and work with me.

This experience so freed me from the bonds of my physical limitations that I no longer felt oppressed by my blindness, but instead soared in the flight of the spirit. I came to see the difference between my body and my "self," accepting completely my powerless-ness over my physical condition. At the same time I ac-cepted responsibility for my spiritual condition: my attitude and the way I live my life.

Although my abstinence had begun on shaky, unsure footing, it grew in strength. As I watched the weeks turn into months and years, I saw my life take on a san-ity and serenity I had never known. In addition, a sig-nificant percentage of my eyesight returned, and today I am able to work, drive a car and do almost anything a fully sighted person can do.

It would not be honest to say that the years in OA have been easy. Stripped of the defense of fat (I now maintain a 40-pound weight loss, down from a top weight of 165) and the rationalizations that let me blame everyone else for whatever happened to me, I have had to confront myself head-on. I have had to deal with my many character defects in the slow and ardu-ous process of growing up.

Many times, there have been food problems. Although I have been abstinent from all refined carbohydrates for more than five years now, the pain of an occasional protein binge has knocked me back down to reality and humility: I am a compulsive overeater; I am powerless over food. I am not proud of this particular learning process, nor do I believe it is necessary for others. It just seems to have been the way for me, and that's all I can share.

I have had to learn to accept myself when I fall short, and rather than become despondent over a slip, to pick myself up again and throw myself with confidence and faith all the harder into working my OA program. I cannot count all the times I have called in my food again to a sponsor for a month or so to get myself back on the track. This helps to remind me that I must remain first, last and always a newcomer in my own mind, and to work my program in that way.

But oh! what treasures I have found through it all. Where once trembled a hurt and frightened little girl now stands a woman with the courage and confidence to live and to love, and to accept what life has to give in return. Through daring to be vulnerable I have been able to form close friendships with many good people, both in and out of OA. And by learning to trust people I have come to trust a God who today is my greatest friend and sponsor, sustaining me through all.

My travels have carried me far, but always I have found the hand of OA stretched out to me. And I in turn have reached out to those who needed me. There is no limit to what can be accomplished in and through the lives of people who partake of the fellowship of Overeaters Anonymous. I know that whatever my future brings, I will be brought again and again into contact with those who can be helped by my experience. And through these contacts, I will be allowed to continue my own progress on this magnificent journey.

28

The Valedictorian

*I*N A FAMILY of painfully thin people, I was labeled the "fat" one. My parents and sisters were so thin they avoided cameras and the females cried after trying on clothes because they were so bony. During the Depression years it was considered healthy to be plump.

When I look at childhood pictures of myself, I realize that I was quite normal. But I thought of myself as fat.

During adolescence I amazed my friends by eating voraciously without putting on a pound; but by high school graduation I was carrying 25 extra pounds, all below the waist, hidden as well as possible by dressing carefully.

The conflict between school and home life was in full bloom. At home I was a clumsy drudge, always striving for perfection (which I thought was possible with a little more effort on my part) and always falling short.

An old French tradition led my parents to seek a balance in our behavior to avoid that most hateful of sins — conceit. The news of any success at school was met with a reminder of failings at home. My self-esteem was very low, although there were moments of great exhilaration — being valedictorian, winning scholarships, cheerleading, election to organizational offices, and important roles in school plays and as a vocal soloist.

My family thought college was a waste of time for a woman, but allowed me to go when I agreed to pay all costs, provide my own clothing, continue with household chores and make a token payment for room and board. What perverse pride I took in being so self-sufficient! The comfortable feeling of martyrdom took the edge off the hardships. Those were busy years. I was hoping to become a woman lawyer, a rare ambition for a steelworker's daughter in post-World War II days.

I worked in a local dairy store, famous for its imaginative creations at the soda fountain. I began to refer to myself as a "foodaholic." It seemed funny then.

After two years my enthusiasm began to wane when one of my friends became an attorney and related discouraging tales of a woman's limited prospects in that field. It was a period of disenchantment for me. College lost its mystique when the academic work proved easy to master, a pattern that was commonplace in my life.

I frankly felt superior to most of the women I knew and had men pegged as an interesting, if unknown, quantity — but certainly intellectually inferior. The men I would have liked to date were put off by my arrogance.

When I began to date often, my parents were concerned about my sexual behavior. Being supersensitive, I took their inquiries as accusations and determined to rebel in my own way. I soon left school, pregnant, to be married. We had three children and a shaky marriage.

I reveled in my "disgrace." I kept friends and neighbors in stitches, pointing out the short-comings of my husband and my misadventures as a housewife. I used to say that I would rather be hated than pitied. Now I realize that my stories were filled with self-pity and all pointed back to "poor me." I loved to help others but would never accept any help for fear that I would then "owe" someone something.

When I was twenty-eight I learned that I had uterine cancer. I had never heard of anyone who survived such a diagnosis and prepared to face death. I wanted desperately to regain my childhood faith but found it out of my reach. I did survive, more confused than ever. The "spayed dog" jokes began and my weight fluctuated wildly. I became overly protective of my children, who were of school age. It didn't take much encouragement to become the forerunner of today's retread college students, this time as a prospective language teacher.

Eventually I was asked to teach at the university level, a position I loved so much I would have paid to do it. Astonishingly, I was never hungry until I arrived home at night. I could easily fast every day until noon, but the minute I opened the refrigerator all resolve melted. In the past, I had read about celebrities who maintained their figures with creative low-calorie dishes prepared by their cooks. If only I didn't have to spend so much time in the kitchen; if only I didn't have to stretch our budget with high-carbohydrate fillers, I could be slim, too.

I gained another 25 pounds which were impossible to hide.

When my youngest son was in high school, I declared
my independence from the kitchen and from any valet
duties in the house. I stated that we were all adults,
that there would be food in the refrigerator, and that
each person was responsible for cleaning up after himself.

I was running out of excuses for my overeating. Even
declaring my independence from the kitchen didn't
stop me.

Then everything fell apart. The industry for which
my husband worked closed its doors. He turned increasingly to drink. Times were changing at the university, too. I was publishing but doomed to perish
without my Ph.D. My husband started at the bottom in
a new job with the merchant marine and suddenly I
was alone and inactive. My weight hit a new high. I
was on my way to becoming fat-lady-of-the-circus
obese.

It was comforting to stay home because I could see
the shock on my friends' faces when I appeared in public. I had always been a chameleon, changing the color
of my personality according to what I assumed was my
reflected image in the eyes of those around me. I hated
that reflection and those who mirrored it. It wasn't the
real me!

But maybe it was. The frayed inseams on my
pantsuits said so. I was falling down often. What had
happened to my figure skater's grace? It came to me
that I had chosen one of the ugliest and slowest ways to
commit suicide.

After experimenting with every diet plan I read
about, I joined a commercial weight-loss group, lost
one dress size, and then despaired. I had heard about
Alcoholics Anonymous and was jealous that they could
attain sobriety while I had to take that first deadly bite
to survive.

I saw an article about OA in *Dear Abby* and sent for information. There was a group in my city. Still, I felt that if I could muster a little self-discipline I could lick the problem. Surely the same drive that had worked so well in school could be channeled into this area.

I had an inspiration. I would make a verbal promise to my husband that when he sailed home again, he would find a thin wife waiting. I could lie to myself, but my word to another was my honor. Oh, how I tried, feeling more hysterical with each failure. My eating was out of control. My hunger was never appeased.

It took me a year to walk into my first OA meeting, humiliated and belligerent. Why should I seek help from a bunch of fatties? (I have since come to love their sensitivity and intelligence.)

"Give me your diet and don't mess with my mind," I told them. They smiled at me. My best sarcasm couldn't penetrate those tolerant smiles. I grabbed some literature. I would read it and judge it and return to tell them how they could improve. Those smiles would evaporate next week.

I lost 26 pounds in the first month and it seemed easy. I kept going to meetings, now smiling back at fellow members with silent smugness.

Unfortunately for my plan to sabotage OA, someone lent me a copy of AA's Big Book. I devoured it in one sitting and began to cry, a feminine weakness I rarely allowed myself. They were telling my story in that book. It took a little translation from alcohol to food, but I recognized myself on every page.

Then my appetite reappeared. I quickly surrendered to it, thinking how little willpower it would take to get started again. But I couldn't get restarted and I learned another truism: It's easier to stay on than to get on.

I went to my next meeting ready to listen to what they were saying about the disease, and it began to make sense — except for some of those twelve steps. How could I have injured anyone? Hadn't my veneer of ladylike politeness prevented me from doing anything worse than using witty sarcasm? Later, when writing my fourth step inventory, I was to discover that my frequent expression, "I hate people who . . . and institutions that . . ." was only the tip of an angry, hurtful internal iceberg.

I began to realize that I had been dieting again and that, unless I made some drastic changes in myself, I would never achieve abstinence. I had to stop analyzing and start acting.

Luckily, I was able to attend a state OA convention where a wise speaker told us that our program was a double trail — without working the step program we would find abstinence impossible and without abstaining we couldn't work the step program well. My mind opened just a tiny crack. I had been afraid to be vulnerable, teachable, but with willingness came many good things.

Recently, I visited a friend who was undergoing treatment for alcoholism. "Aren't you afraid that we are being brainwashed?" she asked. We thought about it for a while and came to the mutual conclusion that our whole past had programmed us into negative thinking and that it would take some welcome "brainwashing" to begin to think positively.

My progress has been terribly slow. Being a quick student in school hadn't helped my plan of action. Often, those whom I sponsor seem to take gigantic leaps forward, inspiring me instead of vice versa. After two and a half years, I have finally lost all but 10 pounds of my excess weight and I have maintained instead of gaining during the plateaus.

My family life has become a great joy to me. What a revelation to find that my husband manages his life much better alone than when it was a joint venture. I simply had to step back to appreciate what he is — a much better person than I was trying to make of him.

My children willingly communicate now without having to defend every action. When I talk with my mother, I know that she has a right to her own actions and that my only responsibility is to love her and control my reactions. Before, the slightest hesitation in her voice told me I had displeased her and threw me into a panic.

I no longer see myself and my world as a reflection in the eyes of others. My perceptions come from a new confidence in my ability to view my surroundings without judgment.

A day of abstinence in my life is a thing of beauty. The fattest abstinent person at a meeting is in a better place than I am if I don't have abstinence.

I have become aware that I have an addictive personality. Maybe that's why I unconsciously denied myself too much liquor, too much impulsive spending.

I find that the void left by all these potential addictions is being filled by the only healthy addiction I have — love. I accept that there is a Power greater than myself and that the love that flows from It enables me to stand ready to love every person with whom I have contact — even the one in the mirror.

It's funny how nice other people have become. On my last birthday I welcomed being forty-eight because physically, spiritually and emotionally I am a much better me than I have ever been.

Someone told me that I have a long way to go if I expect the world to be equitable and fair. I'll never be well, but I am getting better. I have fallen on my face dozens of times, but I can stop branding myself a failure and, with the direction of my Higher Power, pick myself up and grow — a day at a time.

29

First Birthday

*O*NE YEAR AGO, I was facing intestinal bypass surgery and almost certain death. I had suffered congestive heart failure a few months earlier. Following my release from the hospital, where I was put on a strict diet and warned to continue losing weight, I resumed the suicide course of compulsive overeating which soon took me past the 400-pound mark.

Actually, I wanted to die; I had seriously considered taking my life. But I could not do that to my family. With the odds increasingly against a successful bypass operation, however, I saw the surgery as a clean, neat way to destroy myself without scarring my family. I was no good to them or to myself — a useless vegetable of a human being.

I had been a shut-in for six years due to severe colitis. Now, in my extreme obesity, I was becoming more and more helpless. I suffered frequent chest pains. I could not walk. There were days when I could not even brush my hair.

I didn't know it then, but my family did not expect me to live. My son feared what he might find when he got home from work each day. Before leaving the house in the morning, my husband would check me as I lay in bed to see if I was still breathing.

This was my diminishing life that day one year ago as I listened to a talk show on the local radio station. The guests were three members of Overeaters Anonymous. As they spoke, I realized that I was hearing, for the first time, an exact description of my disease.

Then and there I called the station and talked to these good people. They gave me directions and as I listened, I made a commitment of abstinence to myself and my Higher Power.

I didn't hear the entire show; the withdrawal distress was already building and I was becoming dizzy. Whenever this happened, I would immediately eat something — preferably sweets, but if they weren't available, anything would do.

But this day, I *would not eat*! Anxiety pressed in on me. Far into the night, chest pains, stomach cramps and labored breathing kept me awake. I prayed for strength.

At last, a feeling of peace came over me, and with it a strong sense of the presence there in the room with me of OA and all its members. I thought I was hallucinating, but the sensation of not being alone was very pleasant and comforting. I have never been alone since that night.

When I awoke, I thanked God for my first night in OA and my brand new abstinence. With each succeeding day, it became easier to abstain from compulsive overeating. One OA member from the talk show rushed me some OA and AA literature. I was amazed and touched that someone out there cared. I had given up on myself, but these strangers in OA were not about to give up on me.

I read the literature zealously. The AA Big Book gave me great depth of understanding. I sent for OA tapes and listened endlessly, drawing strength from the wit and eloquence of these beautiful, giving people whose lives had been restored to them and who were sharing their abundant gifts in gratitude.

Seven weeks after I began abstinence I got a sponsor, a wonderful woman who has enriched my life beyond measure. She and I talked nightly; we still do, for we have become close friends. In time, I met other OAs who became my friends. They visited me at home and talked with me on the telephone.

In those early weeks, my main source of strength and encouragement was the many telephone contacts with OA members. Get-well cards and letters also poured in. Never have I met more unselfish people than these blessed overeaters. They really are special.

The weight started to come off dramatically at first. From that very first day in OA, my life took a turn for the better in all areas. Even my colitis disappeared, and it has not returned. I was gradually being healed of all that ailed me.

After eight months in the program, a beautiful, almost forgotten world opened up to me: I went out of the house on a shopping trip for the first time in six and a half years! A week later, I ventured forth again, this time for eyeglasses: I had been reading my OA and AA literature with the aid of a magnifying glass.

A few weeks later, I visited my doctor. He was thoroughly astonished and delighted by my weight loss and my greatly decreased blood pressure, which had dropped to 122 over 70. The best advice he could give me, he said, was to keep doing whatever I was doing.

I have had many "firsts" in OA. With my husband, I attended my first movie in twenty years; and I ate in a restaurant for the first time in my life.

The most beautiful "first" by far, however, took place the day I went to my first OA meeting. I, who a year earlier could not carry myself the length of one room, walked tall and straight and free of pain into the very first OA meeting of my life — just two weeks short of one year in the Fellowship.

On my first OA birthday, I weighed myself. I have lost more than 183 pounds; I now weigh 217. In the process of losing weight, I have found a new life. I have experienced the recovery on three levels — physical, emotional and spiritual — that is promised us in the Big Book.

All my life, I floundered about, nearly drowning, in the shipwreck of compulsive overeating. I am still a compulsive overeater, but today my Higher Power gives me a sturdy lifeboat and two strong oars: one of them is abstinence and the other is the OA Fellowship. I am confident that as long as I use these oars, I cannot fail.

30

The Cross-Country Skier

*F*ROM EARLY CHILDHOOD TO the time of my marriage I teeter-tottered up and down the scale. The marriage was unhappy and it ended after five years.

Although my life became happier in the time that followed, in less than two years my weight rose to nearly 200 pounds. A doctor's diet brought it down, but I soon gained it back. I was angry, frustrated and depressed.

About this time I saw an announcement for OA on television. I thought, "I'll have to look into that sometime."

My roommate, who is legally blind, asked me to go cross-country skiing as the driver for a group of blind and partially sighted people. When we got to the ski area we were all fitted for skis and poles. None of us had ever skied before. We were standing in a row waiting to begin, listening to some general orientation from the instructor.

I began to lose my balance. I attempted to maneuver my poles to regain my balance but I fell and in doing so broke a pole. Few of the people around me could see me lying there, disabled as anyone, in a sense. But I felt utterly humiliated.

The rest of the day was a comedy of errors, with the instructor repeatedly saying, "The secret of cross-country skiing is in managing your weight." I became an overnight expert in getting up on skis, since all I seemed to be able to do once I was up was to fall down again.

Many people would consider this experience a "high bottom," and I feel fortunate that it was no worse. When I got home I telephoned the OA hotline and found a meeting to go to.

My Higher Power had been sort of left behind in my life. I was, and am, an atheist. But I certainly do not believe I am the highest power in the universe. I was able to write a description of my Higher Power as "the forces at work in the universe, the interaction of lives within the sphere of one's own existence; chance, luck and the unfolding of every day according to how it will be."

On Easter Saturday I had the first of what were to become many spiritual experiences. The friendship plant my sponsor gave me had been dying by inches. All week it languished and I with it. I loved that plant and would have done whatever was necessary to save it. It was my stepping-up plant and had been for me a symbol of my new way of life.

Someone said it needed water. I had been warned that many people kill their plants by overwatering them and I had carefully tried to avoid that. Still, I gave the plant about a cup of water and put it and my-self to bed. It was lying limp on the soil, its leaves curled up.

I awoke the next morning, the day before Easter, and glanced toward the window. The plant was standing on tiptoe, leaves uncurled, looking healthy and sturdy. Resurrection! A symbol of the sources of my new life: the person who is my sponsor, the person whom I sponsor, Overeaters Anonymous and the Higher Power.

I think by that day I had taken step three, but it was reaffirmed when I turned that poor dying plant over, having done what I could and leaving the rest up to the life force that is a manifestation of my Higher Power.

A year ago I weighed 180 pounds, wore a size 40 swimsuit and was full of negative thinking. I smoked two packs of cigarettes a day and frequently drank a six-pack of beer or three to four highballs at a sitting. I consumed unmeasured quantities of carbohydrates at will. I slept frequently and long — eleven or twelve hours on a weekend night followed the next day by a two-hour nap. I used four-letter words and other pro-fane language frequently. It seemed to fit my chip-on-the-shoulder attitude.

Today I weigh 128 pounds and wear a size 14 misses swimsuit. This is the weight and size I was twenty years ago at the age of twenty. I do not smoke or drink alcoholic beverages, and I swear infrequently and mildly compared to the "drunken sailor" who used to talk out of my mouth. It just doesn't seem to fit my cur-rent lifestyle.

I am a vegetarian. This caused some problems for my sponsors, but I learned that OA is big enough for everyone.

I sleep seven hours out of every twenty-four as my doctor recommended. I get a lot of outdoor activity. This winter, if we can afford it, my roommate and I are going to get cross-country skis. I no longer have to worry about not being able to manage my weight — on or off skis.

As for the spiritual aspect of the program — which for me is the practice of the twelve steps — there is a quotation from the AA book, *Came to Believe,* which I would like to share:

"I know that spiritual growth is a great, wide, beautiful thing and that I have only stepped up to the open door."

For me, that door is OA. I only hope it will open for compulsive overeaters everywhere.

Appendixes

A

A Disease of the Mind

SEVERAL YEARS AGO, as a psychiatrist working in drug abuse and alcoholism programs, I was led through the experience of a staff member to examine compulsive overeating as a disease process identical to alcoholism. We started to apply, in a limited fashion, the same principles to the problem of compulsive overeating that we were using in our alcoholism treatment program, and found them to be very successful. The more closely I examined the phenomenon, the clearer it became that compulsive overeating is a disease.

In medical school, we doctors are never taught about overeating, certainly not as a disease. So we are prejudiced against it. Overeaters Anonymous is very successful with cases that haven't responded to conventional kinds of treatment. This success is often threatening to the professionals because it's difficult for us to see how someone who hasn't had years of study and experience could be more successful with people we've been trying to treat, unsuccessfully, for so long.

The remarkable thing about OA's success is that the program gets people to function far better than they ever have in their lives. With any other disease, you're lucky to get back to where you were. If you have a heart attack, for example, you're fortunate to get your heart to function as well as it did before the attack.

With the compulsive overeater, not only do you get back to a normal weight but, more important, your life is changed and in a sense you're ahead of where you were before you became a compulsive overeater. Now you have tools of feeling, touching, caring, loving, sharing, being honest with your family and looking at life in an understanding way and not fighting it but going along with it. Once you treat the illness, you have the potential for a more "together" person than you were. Therefore, it's exciting for physicians and others who have been ignoring the problem or expressing deep pessimism about it, to think of compulsive overeating as a disease and to realize that it can be treated so successfully.

One of the prejudices about compulsive overeating is society's view of a compulsive overeater as someone who is obese. Yet the overeater can be one pound overweight or even underweight, as in anorexia nervosa, and still be a compulsive overeater. The illness has nothing to do with weight. That's why it's so silly to go on diets or to weigh oneself all the time.

The problem is with the control of food. Is one preoccupied with controlling food intake to the point that it's interfering with one's life? Just as being an alcoholic is not related to the amount one drinks, being a compulsive overeater is not related to the amount one weighs.

The overeater's problem is not being able to control eating behavior the way other people can, and the need is for a system to control that behavior. Of course, the most effective one is a support system like that of Overeaters Anonymous. What the overeater has to do is turn over the control to a higher power. Once it is turned over, the behavior is under control.

A major confusion we in medicine have is the erroneous belief that compulsive overeating is a result of physiologic, psychologic and environmental problems. We try to treat compulsive overeaters psychiatrically or physically with medicine or structures in their lives, and it doesn't work. The reason it fails is because we are doing it in reverse. What has to be dealt with is the compulsive overeating. When it is, the physiologic and psychiatric problems seem to take care of themselves.

There are some people, about the same percentage as in the general population, who, after getting the food back in its proper place, find themselves needing traditional psychiatric care because they do have a problem which they pushed down with food. But that is the exception. What is probably true in most cases is that the individual develops the compulsive overeating mechanism for dealing with life at an early age and then starts to push problems down with the food. Once people become compulsive overeaters, every aspect of their lives is affected. Now they get into the psychological, physical and environmental problems and start changing their lives, their friends and their social structure. All these changes are really caused by the compulsive overeating. Most compulsive overeaters, through a program like OA's, will lose all these syndromes and not need to have any kind of traditional psychiatric care.

We in the medical community must take responsibility for failing to understand the real problem. Compulsive overeating is a serious disease and it is devastating this country. It is the basic cause of disorders which medicine views as primary illnesses, such as hypertension and diabetes. But physicians don't look at compulsive overeating, they look at the secondary disease process which comes from compulsive overeating. They ignore the overeating and rigorously work on the symptoms and the secondary diseases.

Obviously, that is not the way to treat it. If a patient has pneumonia, the doctor doesn't treat the fever and then send the patient home after the temperature is normal, saying "Your fever is down; now watch that pneumonia." But we certainly do this with the overeater. We take care of the symptoms of the secondary disease and we tell that patient, "Your weight (or blood pressure, or blood sugar) is normal; now watch that overeating."

It is the responsibility of the medical community to understand what compulsive overeating really means and to recognize that Overeaters Anonymous has been dealing successfully with the disease. We need to work closely with OA, to have OA as the base or structure, and only then should we offer what we as professionals are able to contribute. The doctor should have the patient go to OA, and then serve as OA's support system for that patient. Overeaters Anonymous should be the treatment and the professional should be the adjunct, not the other way around. This is very difficult for a physician or mental health professional to accept.

As long as Overeaters Anonymous continues to keep the principles it has now, it will be our most valuable means of treatment of the disease of compulsive overeating. OA's principles ensure that no individual has power. In essence, it is a leaderless organization, making the process much stronger than any one member or group.

Overeaters Anonymous is a system of people who are trying to help each other, and as such it is tremendously successful.

WILLIAM RADER, M.D.

Dr. Rader is a psychiatrist engaged in clinical work with alcohol, drug addiction and compulsive overeating. Winner of the 1977 Appreciation Award of Overeaters Anonymous, he has carried the OA message both in his treatment programs and in a number of local and national television documentaries.

B

A Disease of the Body

I WAS MOST PLEASED, several years ago, to be invited as a representative of the American Society of Bariatric Physicians (a medical scientific society devoted to the study of obesity and allied conditions) to attend an annual convention of Overeaters Anonymous. I have since then attended several others. I was also privileged to attend some local group meetings.

The basic concept of Overeaters Anonymous is that compulsive overeating is a disease which affects the person on three levels — physical, spiritual and emotional. Members of OA feel that, like alcoholics, they are unable to control their compulsion permanently by unaided willpower.

Obesity is unquestionably one of the major health problems in the United States today. In fact, it is a problem common to all affluent societies. Estimates as

to the number of overweight individuals in the United
States range from ten million to more than seventy
million, depending on what criteria are used to classify
an individual as obese. Furthermore, in recent years
there has been a steady increase in the number of
overweight individuals. This is due to many factors.
Chief among them is our success in creating an abundant food supply while our physical activity continues
to diminish.

To indicate the magnitude of this menace, a Gallup
Poll in 1973 revealed that 46 percent of Americans
polled felt they were overweight, while less than 8
percent thought they were underweight. Out of every
ten persons, four or five were doing something to control their weight. Senator George McGovern's commit-
tee hearings disclosed that obesity nourishes a ten-
billion-dollar industry, with 100 million dollars yearly
being spent for reducing drugs alone. The U.S. Public
Health Service estimates that at least 60 million Americans weigh more than they should. The most disturb-
ing problem is that perhaps less than five percent of
dieters are able to maintain weight loss for at least five
years.

As a physician, my main concern with the obese is
the medical risks to which their obesity exposes them.
Such persons have a greater than 40 percent chance of
dying in any given year from heart disease, a greater
than 30 chance of dying from coronary artery
disease, a greater than 50 percent death rate from
cerebrovascular disease (strokes) as well as an increased death rate from many other diseases. It has
also been pointed out recently that the risk of developing diabetes is increased twofold by an increase of 20
percent in body weight. In women, there is also a sig-
nificant increase in the development of uterine cancer
associated with excess body weight. In a recent study

of 75,532 fat women, there were sixteen diseases associated with obesity. Furthermore, obesity predisposes to high blood pressure, gallbladder disease and the formation of gallstones requiring surgery. Even babies born of obese mothers have more than twice the infant mortality of babies whose mothers' weights are normal.

Most individuals who join Overeaters Anonymous are aware of these risks. But, like alcoholics, they are unable to control their compulsion on any lasting basis. They have completely lost faith in life and in themselves. In OA, the hand of understanding and strength is extended to them by people who suffer the same compulsion and who are now examples that there is an answer. This probably explains OA's success with the hopeless obese person who has repeatedly failed with the usual methods of weight control. I was particularly impressed with the extreme friendliness and even love between members that was easily observable at meetings.

Many OA members are former participants (and dropouts) of commercial weight control groups. I observed a number of individuals who had been unsuccessful in the commercial organizations, but who had reached and maintained normal weight for a number of years after having joined Overeaters Anonymous. On being asked why they switched organizations, they were quick to inform me that the continual preparation of "free" foods and general preoccupation with food, as sometimes expounded, only kept their food compulsion alive.

When compulsive overeaters realize that they cannot control their eating behavior, they need to accept and depend upon another power — a power acknowledged to be greater than oneself. The interpretation of this power is left to the individual. Many, perhaps most

members of OA adopt the concept of God. But newcomers are merely asked to keep an open mind on this
subject and usually they find it is not too difficult to
work out a solution to this very personal problem, even
if they are atheist or agnostic.

Psychologically, the obese individual is helped to attain a sense of the reality and nearness of a greater
power which replaces one's egocentric nature. Then
the person's point of view and outlook will take on a
spiritual coloring. Hence, one no longer needs to maintain a defiant individuality but can live in peace and
harmony with the environment, sharing and participating freely, especially with other members of the
group. This is a great therapeutic weapon that I, as a
physician who has dealt with obese people for more
than twenty-seven years, can appreciate. The obese
individual no longer defies, but accepts help, guidance
and control from the outside. As OA members relin-
quish their negative, aggressive feelings toward themselves and toward life, they find themselves over-
whelmed by positive feelings of love, friendliness,
tranquility and a pervading contentment. These latter
feelings were evident among the groups I attended.

A word frequently heard in OA groups is *surrender*. It
can best be described as letting go. The individual
gives up personal rigidities, relaxes and admits to
being beaten by compulsive overeating. The source of
this feeling is almost always despair, which is so prevalent in newcomers to the group. It is all part of a crisis
experience with an overload of hopelessness. In the act
of surrender, one does not just give up but accepts a
power greater than oneself, reducing the ego and admitting the need for outside help.

The "ego reduction" can be very profitable to the
personality makeup of this person. It is important to
differentiate between submission and surrender. In

submission, an individual accepts reality consciously, but not unconsciously. There is acceptance that one cannot, at the moment, conquer reality, but lurking in the unconscious is the feeling that "there will come a day when I will be able to handle my problem on my own."

Submission implies no real acceptance of one's inadequacy; on the contrary, it demonstrates conclusively that the struggle is still going on. Submission is, at best, a superficial yielding, with the inner tensions still present. When the individual accepts, on an unconscious level, the reality of not being able to handle compulsive overeating, there is no residual battle. Relaxation ensues with a freedom from strain and conflict. This freedom is the aim of the OA groups, and complete surrender is manifested by the considerable degree of relaxation which is evident in the behavior of those who have achieved it.

Once compulsive overeaters surrender at the unconscious level, their compliance with the disciplines of the program does not lessen with time, leading to the inevitable regaining of weight. They continue to get messages from the unconscious that the need for outside help will remain for a prolonged, if not indefinite period. Their wholehearted cooperation is then forthcoming, and constructive action takes the place of skin-deep assurances that they will merely comply temporarily until the memory of their suffering and self-pity weakens and the need for compliance lessens.

Surrender, then, is an unconscious event. It is not willed by the individual. It can occur only when one becomes involved with one's unconscious mind in a set of circumstances which signal the undeniable need for an external greater power. The definition of surrender can be understood only when all its unconscious ramifications and true inner meaning are glimpsed.

Observed by others, such an individual manifests an inner calm and a "live and let live" attitude.

In analyzing Overeaters Anonymous, I have reached a number of conclusions. There appears to be a deep shift in the individual's emotional tone, the disappearance of one set of feelings, and the emergence of a very different set. The member moves from a negative state of mind to a positive one. This may have the earmarks of a spiritual conversion. Be that as it may, it is an effective transformation and essential for long-term success.

By this I do not mean to imply that there are never any slipups. Indeed, there are. But they are usually due to overconfidence as people are successful in the program and once again become too preoccupied with themselves. As long as they attend group meetings, help is immediately available, inspiring them to return to abstinence and to the twelve steps of recovery. They are neither judged nor scolded. There are no weigh-ins. They can share their past experiences, their present problems and their hopes for the future with those who understand and support them and who speak their own language. Working with a sponsor, the individual converses with a person who has been through similar experiences. Thus the communication between these two is on the same level. When OAs become sponsors themselves, their loneliness is greatly alleviated. They are needed and accepted. This has a very potent, positive influence on weight maintenance.

OA literature suggests that the newcomer visit a doctor to decide upon a plan of eating suited to both physical needs and family habits. I can verify that this was, indeed, the policy with a number of patients whom I have referred to this group. OA is not concerned with the medical aspects of obesity, but with the compulsive nature of overeating.

It is my firm belief that Overeaters Anonymous has made a definite place for itself in helping the obese individual and renders a valuable service to such a person. The empathy and attention individuals receive at meetings during trying times can be of great therapeutic value. Overeaters Anonymous can help individuals restore their faith in themselves and in others and give them hope for recovery. There is no other organization, lay or professional, that has such a profound influence on the compulsive overeater's thinking; and, after all, it is our thoughts that precede our emotions and it is our emotions that make us eat inappropriately and become physically obese. Recovery in OA is on all three levels. It may seem a tall order, but one which has the greatest chance for success.

It has been an honor and a most exciting experience for me as a professional to have had the opportunity to get to know the members of Overeaters Anonymous. I will forever be grateful to them for the good work they do in combating a major health problem in the United States.

PETER G. LINDNER, M.D.

Dr. Lindner is past president of the American Society of Bariatric Physicians and chairman of its board of trustees. He received the 1975 Appreciation Award of Overeaters Anonymous in recognition of his work in the field of obesity and compulsive overeating and his efforts to bring the OA program to the attention of the medical community and the general public.

C

A Disease of the Spirit

*T*HE TITLE OF THIS commentary puts in simple words the uniqueness and special place that Overeaters Anonymous has earned and is earning within the whole approach to the problem of compulsive overeating.

It was not easy to determine how to apply a program dealing with alcoholism, in which thousands have learned how to live without drinking, to a commodity — food — without which no one can live. I am sure that this difficulty still exists within the minds of some. For many others, however, it is clear that what compulsive overeaters and alcoholics have in common is a need to nourish the spiritual side of their nature.

All in all, it is the saving grace of the spiritual in the OA program that has made for its success and growth, and I can prophesy that OA will continue to grow, bringing not only sane eating habits, but spiritually and morally oriented lives that will help build society.

Spiritual values are important because they deal with the whole person. Wholeness in this sense is related to "holiness," as well as to "balance." A holy person is one whose body, mind and spirit share an equality that was (and is) the intention and plan of God for all men. Such a person takes his or her place within the community with ease and grace, motivated by a deep and abiding sense of thanksgiving. Such individuals become creative and constructive, not only with the family circle or community but in the arts and sciences. Their creative energies are not blocked by shame, guilt, self-pity and hate, nor by the facades of arrogance, aggressiveness and uncaring attitudes.

It is only as the hurt and damaged soul is given emotional and spiritual sustenance that these destructive characteristics slough off and love begins to flow freely within and from there outward.

Let us look at this spiritual food. To begin with, it falls under the heading of *love*, the most abused, misused and yet the most wonderful word in the English language. Without love, every other human virtue or ability is as "sounding brass." Love is a spiritual quality that is not confined to the limits of any religious community. No one has a corner on it. It is free — free to fill the lives of all who allow it to flow freely. And as it flows, it both washes and gives life and glorifies its source — God.

This brings me to my first point. Those who are prone to stuff themselves with food that makes their bodies unsightly are refusing the food that satisfies and soothes the unhappy soul within. Have they said, "I don't deserve anything good" for such a long time that they are literally putting their heels on that source of love that alone can bring peace? Or have they become so discouraged or so angry that they deny even the existence of love, let alone God?

All of us can identify with such feelings. Compulsive overeaters and alcoholics, gamblers and drug addicts are not the only inhabitants of life's gray areas. The number of such afflicted people is legion.

There are three stages in the process of getting any kind of food. One: Take your body to the food. Two: Dish it out and eat it. Three: Enjoy it and use the energy it creates. It is the same with spiritual food, food for the soul. Let us look at these three stages.

One: Take your body to the food. Sometimes people become so sick with overeating that the "spiritual food" has to come through one who cares, one who loves. This is God's method. He first loved us. But sometimes He knocks at the door of our lives in the form of a person or a book or magazine article — a thought, a hope.

The knocking is heard but often the door remains shut. Sooner or later, however, it must be opened to allow some kind of help to enter. In most cases, many kinds of "help" have been tried. They all involved money, effort and disappointment. Finally, the message gets through: Someone cared enough to reach the starving soul. You allow love within your life. You are ready to take your body to spiritual food.

Two: This stage follows closely upon the accomplishment of the first. How surprising to find — and difficult to believe — that *all* those people at the OA meeting understood your problem and cared about you!

You see, love that is accepted immediately eliminates your aloneness. The only way you can use the word *love* when you are alone is by loving yourself, and no compulsive overeater does that at first. So it must begin by allowing someone else's love into your life.

This very action of including others and being included is food for the soul — the starving waif within the stuffed body.

But the process of love has only begun. Carefully, even suspiciously, you allow a few people closer to your inner self. Through trusting them, even passively, you move closer to love. You may call these individuals foolhardy to love you, but the pain and loneliness drive you to respond. It becomes easier and easier, until you "overlove" and someone lets you down. This happens because immature love tries to possess and control. Then, you may run back into your shell to lick your wounds, and perhaps a few platters in the process. Like a mighty flood, you feel swamped again by that compulsion that once all but destroyed your life. A phone call: An understanding member of OA hears your story and levels with you. Thankfully, there are many who have learned the difference between loving and "overloving." They are always standing by, ready to help.

What a relief to be on the raft of OA again — that group of people who take you firmly by the hand in love and fellowship.

It is then that you are encouraged to ingest and digest two new kinds of food: First, *understanding* for your straight-jacketed mind. This comes from OA literature and other sources. Secondly, you learn that prayer and meditation have a lot to do with satisfying the inner hungry one. Finally, you can listen to the stories you hear at meetings with a deeper insight. You study the Traditions, born out of pain and trial, which have kept a spiritual movement living and growing for more than forty years. You learn that others have personal histories more traumatic than yours. You acquire humility. You learn some of the tricks of the trade of wholesome living. And finally you can turn to the healthy sauce of good humor. You can not only laugh at the ridiculous reasoning and situations others go through, but you learn to laugh at yourself.

Humor is a most important ingredient of love. I think it shakes down the food — now shrinking away — so that you can make room within yourself for others. This is a major step forward because it takes some of the emotional heat (condemnation) off your self. And what a relief this is!

Fellowship, understanding and humor — all of them digestible forms of love: food for the soul.

Somewhere along this pathway the spiritual itself becomes real to you. You begin to be aware of mystical qualities that become important and real. Is this the birth of a soul? No, because the soul was not dead. It was only starving, denied and stifled. Now it moves within, purring with contentment as it begins its lifelong, God-given task of furnishing control, establishing security and, finally, giving purpose. Now you understand what it was that really attracted you to Overeaters Anonymous. Sure, you were impressed by a slim and trim figure. You wanted that, too. But what really caught you was the love, the understanding, the soul qualities that touched you where you really lived, though you may not have been aware of it.

And wonder of wonders, you too become an instrument of love. You doubted that you could meet the needs of others, but soon the people about you began to respond to your love. Now, you have reached the third stage. You are walking on Cloud Nine, only to be tripped up by pride and even a tinge of complacency or arrogance. The power you envied in others is now yours. You must learn to use it without losing your way again.

Sometimes this experience strands us on a stagnant, arid plateau. You may see someone else maturing more rapidly than you. Disillusionment and standstill can result. There is at this crossroads a signpost you cannot miss: "Go deeper with others and with God."

God has provided many other means of fellowship and growth. They too offer soul-food. But always remember that your compulsion with food does demand that kind of understanding and experience that members of OA can provide. But now that your body is no longer your master, your mind is beginning to think clearly and your soul is fed, nurtured and functioning, you can reconsider those other sources of soul food.

I now leave off my description of this pilgrim's progress which takes us from compulsive overeating to its replacement with food for the soul. It is a journey that leads straight out of self-made prisons and limitations into green pastures where we find many a table spread with wholesome food and a cup that overflows.

THE REVEREND ROLLO M. BOAS

Rev. Boas is a retired minister of the Episcopal church and the recipient of OA's 1979 Appreciation Award. One of OA's earliest supporters, he enthusiastically endorsed the OA program in his pamphlet, "The Compulsive Eater," now in its fifth printing.

D

003 DLY GOVT WHITE HOUSE DC JAN 25
PMS OVEREATERS ANONYMOUS
C/O LOS ANGELES MARRIOTT HOTEL
5355 WEST CENTURY BOULEVARD
LOS ANGELES CALIFORNIA 90045

    I SEND WARMEST GREETINGS TO THE MEMBERS OF OVEREATERS
ANONYMOUS AS YOU CELEBRATE THE TWENTIETH ANNIVERSARY OF THE
FOUNDING OF YOUR ORGANIZATION. I WELCOME THIS CHANCE TO
COMMEND YOU FOR PROVIDING EMOTIONAL SUPPORT AND GUIDANCE
TO THE MANY AMERICANS WHO ARE AFFLICTED WITH THE PROBLEM
OF OVEREATING AND OBESITY.
    OBESITY HAS BECOME A MAJOR PUBLIC HEALTH PROBLEM.
ABOUT TWENTY PERCENT OF ADULTS IN THE UNITED STATES TODAY
ARE OVERWEIGHT TO A DEGREE THAT MAY INTERFERE WITH OPTIMAL
HEALTH AND LONGEVITY. AFTER AGE FORTY, THIS FIGURE JUMPS
TO A STARTLING THIRTY-FIVE PERCENT. THE FEDERAL GOVERNMENT
SHARES YOUR CONCERN FOR THE NUTRITIONAL WELL-BEING OF THESE
CITIZENS AND ENCOURAGES EFFECTIVE PROGRAMS OF RESEARCH
THROUGH WHICH WE CAN IMPROVE OUR KNOWLEDGE OF NUTRITION AS
A BASIS FOR BUILDING BETTER HEALTH AND PRVENTING DISEASE.
    I WISH YOU EVERY SUCCESS AND APPLAUD THE SPIRIT OF
YOUR COMMITMENT TO THE WELL-BEING OF YOUR FELLOW CITIZENS.

       JIMMY CARTER

NNNN

E

The Twelve Traditions

1. Our common welfare should come first; personal recovery depends upon OA unity.

2. For our group purpose there is but one ultimate authority — a loving God as He may express Himself in our group conscience. Our leaders are but trusted servants; they do not govern.

3. The only requirement for OA membership is a desire to stop eating compulsively.

4. Each group should be autonomous except in matters affecting other groups or OA as a whole.

5. Each group has but one primary purpose — to carry its message to the compulsive overeater who still suffers.

6. An OA group ought never endorse, finance or lend the OA name to any related facility or outside enterprise, lest problems of money, property and prestige divert us from our primary purpose.

7. Every OA group ought to be fully self-supporting, declining outside contributions.

8. Overeaters Anonymous should remain forever non-professional, but our service centers may employ special workers.

9. OA, as such, ought never be organized; but we may create service boards or committees directly responsible to those they serve.

10. Overeaters Anonymous has no opinion on outside issues; hence the OA name ought never be drawn into public controversy.

11. Our public relations policy is based on attraction rather than promotion; we need always maintain personal anonymity at the level of press, radio, films, television, and other public media of communication.

12. Anonymity is the spiritual foundation of all these traditions, ever reminding us to place principles before personalities.

Reprinted with permission of AA World Services, Inc., P.O. Box 459, Grand Central Station, New York, NY 10017.

F

To Find Overeaters Anonymous

There are OA groups in all major cities of the United States and in a growing number of smaller communities. Most groups maintain telephone directory listings under "Overeaters Anonymous" and some can also be found in the yellow pages.

Many groups also place announcements giving a local telephone contact number in the classified section of newspapers, under "Personals."

If there are no public listings of OA groups in your area, or if you need information about OA in other countries, write to the World Service Office, 2190 190th Street, Torrance, California 90504.

The international headquarters for Overeaters Anonymous, the World Service Office maintains up-to-date meeting directories, publishes OA literature and provides a broad range of other services for groups, intergroups and regional offices throughout the world.

G

OA Publications

Pamphlets

About OA
A Program of Recovery
Questions and Answers
To the Newcomer
To the Teenager
To the Family of the Compulsive Overeater
A Commitment To Abstinence
The Tools of Recovery
Before You Take That First Compulsive Bite
Sponsors Guide to the Twelve Steps
The Twelve Traditions
OA As Seen by a Doctor
OA Group Handbook
If God Spoke To OA
Introducing OA To the Medical Profession
Welcome Back

Periodical
Lifeline, a monthly magazine

Some literature is available in Spanish. For a complete list of OA materials, please send for an order form from the World Service Office, 2190 190th Street, Torrance, California 90504.